ACKNOWLEDGMENTS TO:

Shirley, my soul mate for 50 years

MW00883143

Why Me, Lord?

Recollections of a Cottonpicker

By

Myron Tassin, 2003

SPECIAL THANKS TO: Denise Tassin Bolt, my sweet niece and Goddaughter for her wise counsel, word-processing expertise, and generosity with her time and talent in bringing order to chaos.

Bernice Ranum, for her secretarial services and for her patience with numerous revisions.

George Wilkinson for computer artistry with old damaged photographs.

Jim and Margie Sparkman, who in the early eighties gave me a typewriter with which to begin this project. The Smith-Corona has long since retired to the landfill, but the challenge lived on.

CONTENTS

PHOTO ID'S

BACK COVER PHOTO BY MICHAEL BEASLEY

Dedication: To Helen

August 10, 1983, Cottonport, LA

We are sitting in my brother's large country kitchen after Mama's funeral and my sister Helen is telling a story. Our faces are gaunt with the exhaustion of a sleepless, 36-hour wake – a somber marathon "rite-of-passage" among the Creole French people of Avoyelles Parish.

Helen's voice falters from the fatigue and emotion of the moment: "On the morning after Joe and I moved in with Pape (pronounced "Pop" as in the French word for "Pope") and NeNan, I heard her calling for us from her bed. Pape was probably already feeding the two or three pigs or milking our only cow.

She continues in a faint voice as if talking to herself as much as to those assembled. "Carefully we approached her bed, not knowing what to expect from this new person in our lives. For the two years since our mother had died, we had lived with aunts and uncles, grandparents, and sometimes with Pape when he wasn't in the fields.

"Her arms spread open on the pillows, she motioned with her hands for us to get into the bed with her, Joe on one side, me on the other. NeNan said, 'I can never take the place of your real mother, but I will take care of you with my whole strength and love you with my whole heart. From now on, you have a real home and a real family!' And then she held us real tight.

"But she was wrong. She <u>did</u> become our mother in every way but birth."

In unison, NeNan's children and stepchildren and grandchildren, friends and neighbors, having gathered that day in that large country kitchen, erupted in subdued sobs…sobs and streaming tears which by all reckoning should have been depleted completely by the grief of the past two days.

Such a tender, loving heartfelt testimony.

Her account of the long-in-coming permanent home sounded like one of those "and they lived happily ever after" stories. And yet, dear Helen, although NeNan and Pape and we five siblings of yours plus your husband, daughter and son-in-law, grandchildren and great grandchildren have all loved you and cherished you throughout the passing years, wounds of uncertainty inflicted upon you from being half-orphaned and "homeless" during your formative years have never fully healed. And for that I am deeply sympathetic.

I like to think that no other brother or sister was closer to Helen than I was. (Of course, self-assurance has never been one of my deficiencies.) Besides helping to raise me, Helen had tremendous influence on the formation of my personality. She pumped more self-esteem into my psyche than a carload of psycho-babbling counselors ever could have.

"Quel un caracter!" (What a personality!), she would say. It is common knowledge that if someone tells you daily how bad you look or asks if you are feeling poorly or if you have been ill, occasionally you will succumb to their powers of suggestion and get sick or at least

Wildon   Helen and Cecile

think you are. Conversely, if someone is always telling you – with sincerity and admiration – how great you are, how carefree you are, you soon will begin to believe it and act accordingly.

Although my Uncle "Bool" (rhymes with "Pool" but I suspect it was a mispronunciation of "bull"), nicknamed me "Hot Shot," it was Helen more than any other who made me feel like one. And I know she loved me more than any other assistant mother ever could.

Fast forward to July 22, 1994. We're in her daughter's home in Baton Rouge, sitting around the kitchen table again. So much good happens around the kitchen table in French families. Food and good conversation are such an integral part of life that the kitchen often is the favorite space in the house.

Helen, her daughter Cecile, son-in-law Kenneth and I are eating boiled crabs from Tony's. A great grandson is munching on a barbecued drumstick.

We're talking about our early years on Bayou Des Glaises at Longbridge, our childhood home. Helen wants to know my earliest recollection of her. She says she can't remember when I was born although she remembers the coming of the other three in the "second family." Maybe I was hatched.

Smiling broadly, she waits for an answer. I tell her I believe it was in the kitchen (yes, again) at the old sharecropper's house – lá maison a Reggie (the house owned by our landlord, Reggie Coco).

I tell her I remember her debating rather vehemently with my mother who is ironing some shirts. She is begging to go to our Uncle Edward's house down the road. Mama says she can't because she knows why Helen wants to go there. I am three or four and Helen is about 15 and I'm perturbed to see my mother and sister going at it verbally. The discussion is as hot as the summer kitchen, with the wood stove blazing away to keep Mama's black irons hot.

Helen says she might go anyway. "If you do, you'll have to answer to your father when he comes in from the fields." Helen complains bitterly like any other thwarted teenager, but she doesn't go. Obedience wins the day.

Through the years, I had heard that, during her teens, Helen had a scorching crush on her first cousin, Edward Tassin, Jr., known to all as "Mulatre," French for Mulatto. Although he had dark black hair, the handsome young man had contrasting alabaster-white skin, just the opposite of a Mulatto's brown tones. So they called him "Mulatre" like you would call a large man "Tiny."

The pretty smile leaves her face abruptly when I tell her, "I believe Mama said you wanted to go see a boy." I'm watching her twinkling eyes...looking for confirmation.

"He's dead," she responds without preamble nor explanation of any kind.

"So there was a boy?"

"Yes, he's dead."

The boy was Mulatre who died on the beach at Normandy in June of 1944. I understand they were inseparable when opportunities presented themselves at neighborhood dances, family visits, chance meetings...probably a few arranged meetings. They talked of eloping...of other strategies to assure marriage wouldn't be blocked.

The grownups evidently were successful in keeping the two apart until the heat of the moment cooled off. How sad that her first true love would be denied. Almost as sad as her biological mother passing away during her childhood.

Deep wounds, both.

A man of small stature, Wildon was a wonderful husband. They looked good together. "Petit" and "Petite," they should have been called. Helen has consistently weighed around 100 pounds while Wildon, nicknamed "Malaille" (for what reason I know not), tipped the scales at 135 when his pockets were stuffed with automotive repair tools, the implements of his trade.

Good and kind and happy, he certainly was a fine brother-in-law to me. When he lay dying from throat cancer, I sat on his bed and cried with him. I wrote a letter telling him what our friendship had meant and how good he had been to me. I reminded him of the time I worked at his service station when I had borrowed, in his absence, from the day's receipts to play a slot machine in the grocery store next door. Without preaching, without rancor, he had simply deducted the small sum from my next paycheck.

Over a period of five years, as her partner suffered the gruesome ravages of his illness, she endured all that was thrown at her with courage and strength and undying love. Mulatre might have been her first love; Wildon was surely her life-long love.

She followed him to Kansas and Michigan during the war, with the latter time requiring the heart-wrenching decision to leave her infant daughter with us so she could eke out a few more weeks with him before his shipment to the Philippines, perhaps never to return. "Hon" they called each other, and it was indeed a sweet, syrupy romance throughout their 39 years of marriage.

While he was overseas, she lived and worked with us in the harsh cotton fields. I did her little notions shopping at Mr. Gano's Grocery across the street from Cottonport school: Jergen's Lotion, Q-Tips, baby oil, talcum powder, Tichenor's Antiseptic, Ipana Toothpaste, Black Drought, candy, cookies... Every time, I would get a tip. The funds came from her military dependent's allowance.

I remember shopping for the makings of a picnic she was planning to throw for us: a six-pack of strawberry pop, some vanilla cookies topped off with marshmallows and a sprinkle of coconut, a pack of Kits and one of Mary Janes.

She took us to the peach tree orchard adjoining our yard. It was hot and humid. Swarming insects were in their prime. Still recovering from the depression of the thirties, we were not used to store-bought sweets, so we were excited. In five minutes we had gulped down all of the goodies and chased them down with tepid red pop (we had no electricity and no ice but the bottles were immersed in a tub of cool well water).

Flies were buzzing, mosquitoes were biting, humidity was soaring. The grand picnic to which we had all looked forward with great expectations was gone in a flash, and we retreated to the security and relative comfort of our screened porch. The party was a bust, but Helen had done it for us when her heart was surely heavy with loneliness and worry for her husband who was half a world away in hostile circumstances.

Sweet Helen, together for these 69-odd years, we have lived and loved, laughed and cried, picked cotton and enjoyed strawberry pop and boiled crabs. And for a brief time during our visit a week ago, your sweet smile told me that the hurt stretching back to your tender years is sometimes, somewhat soothed. In fact, I definitely saw traces of peace in the well-earned lines of your face. Could it be that the wounds have finally healed and that I am seeing only well-healed scars? Could it?

At Joe's funeral on April 20, 1994, the weight of the moment must have been ponderous for you. Mother, father, stepmother, husband, two brothers...all gone. Still you have rebounded with a resilience that testifies to your faith, courage and fortitude.

To Pape's "Cherie" (his favorite name for you), I say, "WELL DONE!"

INTRODUCTION

Why is my sweet and smart daughter, Anne, pressing me to write about our family, our friends, our roots, and life? Is it because she sees my hair falling out like gray rain, or could it be that my wrinkles are themselves getting wrinkles while the wrinkles on my brain are growing smooth?

An acquaintance of mine pledged on his 53rd birthday to hike up to the peaks of each of Colorado's 53 over-14,000-foot-high mountains; it took three years. I thought about doing that, but who wants to be a copycat?

On this, my 69th birthday, I pledge to finish this project soon. There now: this definite equivocation makes me feel better.

For at least a decade, I have been making idle threats about launching this venture and actually began piddling with it about four years ago. However, sister Helen gave me a good excuse to put it away when she expressed discomfort with my telling about her "forbidden" teenage romance (see Dedication).

Thankfully, on a recent visit to Baton Rouge, she finally gave me her approval (with witnesses present), and I am most grateful to be able to include this innocent story of love, denial, war and death. It's the only intrigue in the whole book, so I felt I had to have it.

Should this tome convey spiritual overtones, I make no apologies. My life to this point has been such a series of serendipitous chapters, it could hardly be a matter of chance; there has to be a Greater Hand in all of this, so I often ask myself, in a positive frame, "Why me, Lord?"

For one thing, my life has been spared several times: from surviving a plane crash while attempting a gear-up landing on a Colorado gravel airstrip; a near-drowning, after being knocked senseless in Florida waters; being run over and dragged on a Louisiana road by a Model A Ford traveling about 35 miles per hour; a motor home flip-over in a Texas ice storm...not to mention complications after an encounter with a cardiologist's knife in quadruple bypass surgery at Cedars Sinai Hospital in Beverly Hills, California. You must admit that, geographically speaking, I do spread my close calls around.

This book is not a commercial venture; it is something to leave behind for my family, friends and my progeny who, when they ask their parents about the "olden days," will be given a copy of this as a primer.

Because I don't have to please the publisher, I can afford the luxury of doing it <u>MY</u> way. It is not chronological; it jumps around with segments that would fit well into the "Oh, I forgot to tell you" category.

The title, "Why Me, Lord?," came to me at Mass one day in another moment of inattention to the service at hand. While it can have positive as well as negative connotations, (i.e., "How do I deserve to be so fortunate, Lord?" or "Why all this bad luck, Lord?"), the positive aspects will occupy most of the space because most of my life has been free, fulfilling and joyous, and I'm looking forward to more.

Oh, another title considered was "Black and White Rainbows," a line extracted from a "poor joke" I have enjoyed repeating to wealthy friends. ("We were so poor during the depression, the rainbows over my house were in black and white.") It is clever and an attention getter, but surely misleading because most of my rainbows have been in vivid, sparkling colors.

For those of you who don't want to be bored by this vain, personal exposé, the highlights – although not very"high" – are pretty much enumerated at the end of this intro; thus, once you read them, you can put away this "autobabbleography" for GOOD, without wasting any more of your precious time. Okay?

Since I don't know where to begin, I shall commence from the start, so here goes:

BRANCHES: ("Roots" has been co-opted.) The name Tassin can be found in French history as early as 980 AD. Our family tree is documented back to the 1600's, thanks to Rosemary Ducote Rachal, my second cousin, who compiled an extensive, impressive detailed genealogical search of the Tassin and Ducote (my mother's maiden name) families.

Call it the luck of double first cousins, but this is how it happened: Rosemary's grandmother was Winnie Tassin, my father's sister, and her grandfather was Willie Ducote, my mother's brother. Hence, when she did the research for her grandparents, she did it also for my parents.

A marvelous, massive job it is, stretching to 89 typewritten pages and reaching back over 300 years. To her we are all deeply indebted.

Her work enables me to tell you that my great, great, great, great, great paternal grandparents were Francois Tassin and Marie Roy of Mercey, France, which is located about 12 miles from Eureux, which is some 50 miles northwest of Paris.

Joseph Tassin, their only known child, came directly from France to New Orleans in the early 1720's; thus, we are not Acadians, or "Cajuns," who migrated from Acadia in Nova Scotia, Canada, to Louisiana between 1735 and 1755. We are FRENCH directly from France!

THE FARM – Although times were tough during the depression, we were blessed with a virtually self-sufficient farm. We were poorly clothed, but we ate well. Our medical and dental care were lacking, but we ate well. We had no money, but we ate like royalty! And if you know French people intimately you know that good food ranks near the top of life's pleasures.

The chapter about growing up on a small, balanced, fecund farm during the thirties contains much of the meat of this book.

L'ACCIDENT – After being dragged for about 100 feet on gravel, the only broken body part was my head. Soooo, now you know why I'm a little strange.

SCHOOL – I went to a public school that was in many ways like an exclusive private one, run by outstanding staff and teachers with compassionate but strict discipline which gave you, in my eyes, a student body with an esprit de corps sans pareil.

I liked school; it was so much better than farm work. My classmates are treasured friends to this day, 50 years after graduation.

WORK – I began picking cotton at age six and abhorred every minute of my 12-year career in that "field." I have since had four employers and founded three businesses, all of which were considered vacations compared to my first "position."

COLLEGE – A high school teacher pointed me toward a degree in journalism and a career therein; what a tremendous gift. Thank you, Madeline Cassidy Ducote.

BOOKS – I drifted into becoming an author of several mostly inconsequential, non-scholarly, non-fiction books which provided the basis for a life with abundant freedom, enjoyment, continuing education and enough income to pay the basic bills.

LAND – As a reluctant son of the soil, I began appreciating its value and began investing in it in 1960.

The EARLY MEMORIES chapter is boring with subjects like garlic breath, a remembered spanking, killing the Easter bunny, state of the art toys, a stingy Santa, real gypsies, bonafide Mardi Gras bandits…you know, the run of the mill stuff. Next, you will be spellbound with the chapter on LA GRANDE FAMILLE. With Mama and Daddy's 26 siblings, it was really grande. You'd better like the chapter on my mother's artistic expression, or else. GOING AWAY…AND STAYING is about leaving home on the morning after high school graduation, still infected with a strange bug known to be found in assorted bottles at the Blue Moon Club in Bunkie. You'll read about a series of miracles in my one and only HUNTING

<u>ADVENTURE</u> with my father. There's a lot about living in the mountains and living by the sea and parts in between. You'll learn the difference between Creole and Cajun and how it feels to be French. In my brilliant military career, you will see how I almost got the purple heart.

In a serious vein, I conclude with a profound failure in my life, and then I pay tribute to my soul mate of 50 years.

You've read about the highlights; now you can put it away…unless you want to read about some really stupid things I've done. Ah-haaa! Gotcha!

BRANCHES

My great, great, great, great, great paternal grandparents were Francois Tassin and Marie Roy of Mercey, France. Their only known child, Joseph, also of Mercey, was the first Tassin to emigrate to America (1720) and is the progenitor of our Tassin family in the new world.

Irma Lacour, wife of my grandfather, Adolphe Tassin, was a descendant of Nicolas Lacour who, in 1718, came to New Orleans from St. Jean des Champs, Bishopric of Contenac, France. He sailed aboard the vessel "Compte de Toulouse."

On my mother's side, Pierre Ducote I, born in Flanders, France, around 1691, was the progenitor of the Ducotes of Avoyelles Parish and Louisiana. The Ducote name is believed to be exclusively of Avoyelles Parish, not having been found to be among the family names in other parts of colonial Louisiana.

The genealogy of American Ducotes is as follows: Pierre Ducote I, my great, great, great, great grandfather, was the father of Pierre Ducote II, who begat Joseph Ducote, who begat Pierre Ducote, who begat Pierre Amable Ducote, my grandfather. Pierre Amable and Louise Dubroc Ducote were the parents of my mother, Emma Ducote Tassin, and nine other children.

On the Tassin side, the genealogy is as follows: Francois Tassin and Marie Roy, my G-5 grandparents, begat Joseph Tassin, who begat Nicolas Tassin I, who begat Nicolas Tassin II, who begat Jean Baptiste Tassin, who begat Anatole Tassin, who begat my grandfather, Adolphe Tassin. Adolphe and his first wife, Irma Lacour Tassin, were the parents of Pliny Tassin who married Emma Ducote and became my wonderful parents.

Grandfather Adolphe produced 16 children. He and Irma Lacour had nine. My father Pliny was number eight, the last son in that first crop. After Irma's death, Grandpapa remarried and this second union produced one child. Following his second wife's death, he married Louise Guillot, and they had six children.

Grandpapa Adolphe was a slight man with white hair and a prominent mustache of the same color, which he would twitch all over my face, a farcical routine which led to much giggling and sneezing on my part. I remember the day he was buried and I was very confused about grown-ups crying.

During the 300-plus years between the late seventeenth and twenty-first centuries, beautiful French family names appear in the Tassin-Ducote bloodlines; some are: Bordelon, Bissette, Bouchard, Baudet, Biget, Bellanger, Bonnet, Bourgeois, Chatelain, Chevalier, Champagne, Charpain, Cellier, Colon, Casse, Decuir, Dubroc, Duclos, Decour, Delehante, Dubos, De Brachon, De Muisse, Edelme, Enet, Etienne, Fondilique, Hennet, Joffrion, Juneau, Laurent, Lemoine, La Casse, Le Breque, Marssine, Marcotte, Mayeux, Moreau, Milot, Normand, Pelletier, Pebos, Pilois, Phillippe, Prevost, Rabalais, Roy, Rondot, Roland, Sanmerine, and Simon.

If you know how to pronounce them, you know how lyrical, musical, and FRENCH they sound.

EARLIEST MEMORIES

There are those who say that one's early memories begin at three or four, claiming that if you go back earlier than that, you're remembering incidents which have been related to you by others. I disagree completely.

One of my earliest recollections goes back to the birth of my sister, Mary Ann, who was born when I was just about to turn two. On a cold, rainy day, Joe, Helen, Bobby and I were herded onto the back porch. We could see Daddy in the kitchen, probably boiling the proverbial pot of water and ripping sheets. Several ladies were with Mama. I will never forget her horrible cries of agony; I thought they were hurting her on purpose.

Other early memories include:

Riding in the buggy to Mass in Mansura on winter Sundays with feet planted firmly on heated bricks wrapped in an old blanket, and the stench and steam generated when our old steed would relieve himself on the singletree and harness. The stern stares from Mama when we guffawed too much.

An apple in one shoe and an orange in the other as tokens of Santa's largesse. (Note: I never cared much for the bearded ole elf because I had heard that he could do anything, but when it came to presents from him to me, he acted like we were in the middle of the Great Depression. If he could fly through the air with a sleigh full of goodies, why couldn't he bring me that shiny red and white bicycle, the one I dreamed about incessantly?)

Raindrops falling on our heads during thunderstorms. Pots and pans pitter-pattering all over the house.

The cozy fun of sleeping like silk worms, surrounded by the veils of mosquito nets.

Sucking my milk-spiked-with-syrup bottle under the dining table with my feet propped up on the leg braces. I understand I suffered from anemia at two so my mother supplemented my diet with this turbo-charged concoction.

Taking a turn around the yard with my "horse," a coke bottle with string for bridle and reins.

The little red ball I received from my godfather...the only gift I remember ever getting from him.

Malou, an old maid (at the time) relative, fighting to rock me to sleep after Sunday dinner, and her garlic-scented burps. Did she love me that much, or did she hate to do dishes?

Slipping out of the yard, getting lost in the contiguous cotton patch and being found by our little dog, followed by a band of searchers led by a tearful mother.

Escaping from the front yard to run and meet Daddy in his buggy, and the resulting red posterior.

Fighting with Bobby for a turn at cranking the Victrola handle at weekend dances for Joe, Helen and friends.

The family literally sweeping the yard, laid bare of growth by hungry fowl.

Annual floods, marching from the back woodlands through the fields and to our yard and house, and the night Daddy used a hoe to chop up a water mocassin which had set up digs atop the armoire.

Taking a quart bucket of biscuits and syrup to Joe for a mid-afternoon snack in the field, and the time he told me he had caught the Easter Bunny and had eaten all of the candies in his little wagon, showing me the candy stains on his hands as "proof." Being too young or dumb to notice that the handles of his plow were red and leaching color on his perspiring hands.

On Mardi Gras, a band of hooded masked horsemen, riding through our yard and scooping up precious hens with dip nets for their gumbo that evening. There were rumors that sometimes these brigands would net bad children, so we hid under the beds.

And then, there were the gypsies. Until the mid-thirties, horse and wagon caravans of tinkers would roam the land, camping on federal properties like bayou banks and levees. I remember our family attending their little weekend festivities near the new, long bridge (the old one had washed away during the catastrophic flood of 1927) where the gypsies sold trinkets, repaired your pots and pans and invariably beat you out of a few pennies in carnival-like games.

One night, I remember the horses whinnying loudly at our barn across the road. My father figured they must be stealing his hard-earned corn in the crib, so he ran to the porch and shot his 12-gauge long-barrel Savage in the direction of the activity. When the BB's struck the tin roof, a loud commotion followed, with noises coming from barbed wire along the bayou bank. Next morning, Daddy found torn clothing on the fence, and the caravan was gone, never more to return.

For many years, parents would motivate their children by warning, "Next time the gypsies come, we might put you on the wagons with them."

Finally, the encounter with a savage world.

My parents were deeply religious, especially my mother, whom I liked to call a "lay nun." So you can imagine her consternation when I had my first brush with the dark side.

My brother, Bobby, and I were walking to a small store located where our gravel road met the "black top" road to Mansura to pick up what meager items a few eggs would barter for, and we ran into a young ruffian named R. D. Armand, who asked us where we were going.

"We're going to buy some bologna"(we called it baloney).

"You eat that stuff?" he asked in French. "That's terrible stuff," he continued.

"Mais oui," we responded proudly. "We like it very much."

"C'est du cue de mulet," R. D. insisted.

When Bobby, always the good child, reported our brief conversation – which we didn't understand – to "Sister Emma," she turned red as a beet and fumed. It seems that cue de mulet in anatomical terms could be described as a body part of a mule located just south of where the tail bone is connected to the backbone.

Alas, R. D. had contaminated her innocent little angels. She probably said some purification prayers over our beds that night.

_ Left to right, top to bottom: Brother Joe and wife, Olive; Beryl Ducote Robin, Olive's niece and my classmate; Daddy and Mama, brother Sidney; Ronald and Sharon, Joe and Olive's children.
_ Myron, brother Bobby, sister Mary Ann (looking down), Sidney held by Helen.
_ Bobby, niece Cecile Mayeux held by Myron, Sidney and Mary Ann.
_ Sidney looking left, Bobby, Daddy holding granddaughter Cecile, Myron and Mary Ann. (Mama must have been the photographer)

THE PLINY TASSINS

My father's first wife, Angella Desselles, died in 1927 at age 30 from a ruptured appendix, leaving him with a nine-year-old son, Joseph, and Helen who was seven.

In those days, the only childcare "agencies" were those staffed by family; a dirt farmer could hardly drag the little ones behind a plow. Consequently, the two siblings gravitated between grandparents and aunts and uncles.

In 1929, my mother was working in New Orleans as a seamstress. On one of her infrequent visits to Cottonport, her brother and Daddy's sister – man and wife – introduced them to each other. Daddy was the marrying kind and needed a mother for his children; Mama, at 33 years of age, was a prime candidate. During a brief courting season, they got along famously, as they say, and were married within months. They were nuts about each other, each giving much more than expected.

Daddy was a rough, gruff taskmaster, but he had a heart of gold and was extremely sentimental.

As far as I am concerned, everything he meted out in the way of discipline or showed in disappointment in me was truly deserved. The fact that I was a misfit as a farmer's son should in no way be construed as a failing on his part, no matter how much I may complain about it.

Mama was patient in the extreme, generous, loving, selfless, devout, energetic yet slow in motion, sweet, joyful in an understated way, dedicated to the family, self-sacrificing and hard working.

In Daddy's second crop, Bobby was born in 1931, yours truly in '33, Mary Ann, '35 and Sidney in '39.

I remember Joe in his youth as a quiet, withdrawn teenager, but he certainly made up for his shy and insecure period in his adult years as he became a self-assured extrovert. His friends will tell you it was great fun to be with him. I agree wholeheartedly. A serious, successful farmer, he was devoted to caring for his wife throughout his and her long years of illness.

A 93-pound dynamo, Helen (see Dedication) was an introspective person whose youthful hardships seemed to linger just below a pleasant surface. While her personality could be described as cautious, in times of celebration, she was joyous, generous and carefree.

I can honestly say that none of us, least of all my parents, ever treated anyone from either crop as less than fully enfranchised. I saw Joe and Helen as my full – not half – brother and sister – period.

Bobby was serious, industrious, mature beyond his years, intensely religious, a natural engineer, the problem solver on the farm. He perfected an efficient rabbit trap which supplemented our diet during the Depression. He taught himself how to re-cover and re-sew softballs for the school sports program as well as for individuals who could afford his handsome fee.

As flighty, unreliable and impulsive as his closest brother was, Bobby was a reliable, methodical, accountable man/boy. He was profoundly intelligent, especially when he married Jean; together they raised six outstanding children. Jean was always kind and loving to my parents and always "there" for them. She cared for Bobby tenderly and diligently for the 14½ years between his first stroke and his death.

Although Bobby hadn't felt the intense sibling rivalry I had experienced with a brother two years my senior, I broached the subject with him on one of our great hunting trips in the Colorado mountains, and he was quite generous with his understanding.

A tomboy from the get-go, Mary Ann was totally immersed in softball – a game where her diminutive size was no major impediment (remember Peewee Reese?). They called her "Tee," presumably from the French word "petite." When she entered the batter's box, the stadium would hush in anticipation. Pound for pound, she was one of the best hitters on her high school team. She didn't necessarily hit 'em far, but she hit 'em often. She spent her whole business career hitting homers in computer science for the Louisiana Department of Highways. We have grown even closer during our "middle" years.

To me, her most enduring character traits are her sense of humor and wit. She can keep you in stitches, patches and seams for hours on end.

Mary and friend, Marlene Courville of Krotz Springs, have been living in Baton Rouge for 48 years. Their Cajun cooking is art itself.

When Shirley called me at Fort Bliss, Texas, to tell me that Sidney, my 16-year-old brother, had been killed as a passenger in a pickup truck accident, I thought I'd never get over it and, if I did, my elderly parents surely wouldn't. But time and faith proved me wrong on both counts.

As of this writing, he's been gone for 46 years – so long, in fact, that I go several days now without thinking about him. For years after his death, I found it extremely difficult to fall asleep without dwelling on him and the tragedy. He was a good boy, loved by all, who didn't have it all that easy with elderly parents who tended to be a little over-protective.

Of the five males in our family, including Daddy, I am the sole survivor – which makes for a serious, necessary confrontation with mortality and the downslope of a good life. To see some of my youngest grandchildren graduate from high school, I would have to live to my mid-eighties. Why not? Mama made it that far; however, with my share of close calls, I fully accept the admonition that one does not know the day or hour. THY will be done.

Emma Ducote Tassin

Pliny Adolphe Tassin

Bobby, Joe, Mary Ann, Myron

LA GRANDE FAMILLE: RELATIVES

As a child, one of the first complex realities I encountered was that of our extended family including grandparents, aunts and uncles, nieces and nephews, and cousins to the second and even third degree of kindred.

Perhaps I never learned who all of my third cousins were, but I knew my first and second. With Mama coming from a family of 10 children and Daddy from a brood of 16, there were plenty to remember, but it was something driven into us like the American Indians' custom of retelling their history from generation to generation.

La famille was of utmost importance. On any given Sunday, any number of my mother's siblings, spouses, and their children would meet, greet and eat at my grandparents' home. They would arrive uninvited. There were no phones and little transportation to let your host know you were coming. For special occasions like holidays, my uncle, school bus driver Filtz Laborde, was the note carrier.

The get-togethers were grand pot-luck affairs. They were like major holidays on an ordinary Sunday. For a child it was heaven, with playmates like Judy, Sherrel, Ronald, Sylvian, Eloise, Raymond, and Amy Louise in a wide ranging age group.

PaPa Ducote was well regarded by one and all. He had a small grocery store in the corner of his yard, located at the junction of two roads and two bayous: Rouge and des Glaises.

On Christmas morning, PaPa would sit in his big rocking chair in front of a roaring fire to receive well-wishers who came from near and far on foot and horse. It was a scene not far from the contemporary "Godfather" movies excepting this was <u>my</u> "Grandfather," and he was truly "grand."

They would come into the living room, shake his hand and retreat to the hearth with their backs to the fire.

"Je voudrais vous souter un joyeau 'Cristmees' et une bonne annee," they would say. The dignified, mustachioed gentleman would invite each to have a small shot of whiskey with him. By dinnertime, his cheeks were glowing.

Fiercely independent and active, he spent his last day searching for a missing cow. Several people saw him in town (a couple of miles from home) looking for his bovine. In Louisiana climatological terms, it was an unusual below-freezing day. That afternoon he was found frozen stiff in a ditch near his home. He was 77.

When my uncle, the bus driver, came to get his first load, word spread among the grandchildren like wildfire. There must have been over a dozen of us standing around in shocked disbelief. First word was that he had frozen to death, news that sounded too bizarre and horrible to believe. Freezing to death just didn't happen in central Louisiana. The coroner, I believe, found that he had had a stroke or heart attack.

As I waited for the second load, I thought of my mother who was profoundly fond and respectful of her father. I knew she would be grieving deeply.

It is a gross understatement to say that I dreaded the wake that would take place that night at my grandfather's home. It was the custom in French-Catholic Louisiana to mourn the dead demonstrably.

One daughter of the deceased would approach the coffin and begin to cry, "Oh, mon cher, en va te manquer." "Oh my dear we will miss you." "Pauve vieu chien, il devait etre froid quand il a tomber, ét il etait tout seul." "Poor old puppy, he must have been cold when he fell, and he was all by himself."

Another sister would come to the coffin to lead the other one away lest she be consumed by grief, but she herself would fall into the pattern of displaying her love, devotion and consummate sadness; crying and wailing would erupt in the audience as a show of support. Every time someone entered the house to offer sympathies, the process would flare up again like a flame on a conifer log full of pitch. At 3:00 A.M., I went to an aunt and uncle's house across the road and collapsed, emotionally and physically spent, on a cold bed.

Like the Muslim women you see in the funeral processions, our mothers, sisters, and aunts did much the same. One of my aunts could have been qualified to be a professional mourner; my brother felt she could have earned a good living at it.

Although it was not considered a manly thing to do, French men were apt to cry at wakes when emotions reached surging heights, but seldom did you see one lose control.

I'm not being critical of Creole mourning; psychiatrists tell us now that it is a helpful avenue in the long journey of facing and

17

accepting the loss of a loved one, a bromide bringing closure. However as a child with a deep and abiding faith, I felt that these fervently religious women were somehow not agreeing with God's decision to call someone to be with Him. Right or wrong, I felt they were saying, "I believe in You and your message, Lord, but I can't believe You would be so thoughtless as to take this loved one from our midst." I expressed this to my mother when she went into the traditional six-month period of mourning, with no make-up, solid black dress, and no music.

On one hand we were taught that, at death, as soon as a soul leaves for other parts, the body is nothing. Yet, for hours, even days, they stood around the coffin talking to the body that was supposedly nothing without its spirit, an empty vessel…a very confusing message for a child.

Adolphe Tassin

Maternal Grandmother Louise Dubroc Ducote

THE FECUND FARM

Until I was five years old, we lived on a small tenant farm in Longbridge, Louisiana. My father worked his little patch from daybreak to about 7:30 A.M., then went with his horse to his WPA (Workman's Progress Administration) job, a sort of workfare program. His pay: $1.00 a day, horse included. After work he returned to his few rows of cotton and corn. The WPA employment had the farmers building a flood-control levee on Bayou des Glaises – not with machines – but with horse and scraper. It was "make work," but the consequences were positive as the levee system ended the spring floods which had perennially ravaged the fields of the French settlers. Too poor to afford a pair of cheap gloves, he would come home with blistered, bloody hands.

It can be accurately said that in my short life span of 69 years, we have gone from horses and buggies to SUVs, to jet travel, to the moon, to planetary probes; from kerosene lamps to halogens; from cistern water collected off tin roofs to today's filtered Britta systems; from wood stoves to microwaves; from food preservation in jugs lowered into cold springs to temperature-controlled refrigerator freezers; from counting on fingers to magical computers and calculators. Our life spans have zoomed from 50-something to the mid-seventies.

My father was not quite as devout as Mama, but he said his rosary daily and his prayers on his knees nightly, went to Mass every Sunday and received Communion almost every Sunday. In about 1937, Daddy became proactive with prayer when he and several men in the neighborhood walked to Mansura for several nights in a row to make a novena asking God's intercession that they might escape the harsh poverty of the Depression. Soon after, the government introduced a program of low-interest loans akin to today's disaster relief.

Daddy borrowed $5,000, bought a 40-acre farm just a mile and a half from our tenant acreage (from which half of your crop went to the landowner) and built a three-bedroom home (no bath). We moved there on my first day in the first grade. Don't worry about the "no bath" part; we had a small room in the house where we bathed in a number 3 washtub. The "restroom" part was accommodated by a breezy two-holer in the far corner of the backyard.

The new house was paradise. It didn't leak, the windows had screens, the large pantry was always full of preserves (vegetables and fruit), and we lived merrily on. But still there was NO money! In spite of that minor complication, we lived well. We had little clothing, but except for salt, refined sugar, flour, rice and absolutely necessary medical attention, we were pretty self-sufficient.

On the farm, corn was the main force in the chain of life, somewhat like it was for the Aztecs and Incas of old. Of our 40 acres, seven were devoted to cotton, our cash crop, and about eight acres to corn and soybeans, and the balance to grazing. Our farm sat on deep, rich alluvial soil, brought down to us on the Mississippi plain by eons of annual floods. So we made up to two bales an acre while the northern part of Louisiana needed several acres to produce one. An average 500-pound bale, at 10 cents a pound brought $50 and the seed paid for the ginning. Multiply that by 12 bales and you had amassed a fat gross budget of $600 for the coming year. Sale of a couple of grade calves and several litters of piglets, plus a few sacks of soybeans, brought that up to $800 for the year...if the weather had cooperated with the cotton crop.

We didn't need much. The corn fed a horse and a mule that pulled the plows and the wagon. It fed the hogs that gave us fresh pork, sausages, hogshead cheese, andouille, gogue (stuffed pig's stomach), ham smoked in a tiny room in the chicken house and salt meat for seasoning veggies. The joke was that all we lost when we butchered a pig was the hair and the squeals. We even saved the blood to make boudin, a rice, organ meat and blood dressing stuffed into the cleaned intestines. Yuck!, you say? If I blindfolded 10 people and they had no preconceived notions and prejudices, I predict a large majority would pick these sausages over most other fine foods. Note for the squeamish: remember, before you take the feathers off of a wet spring chicken, it's pretty yucky.

We butchered a pig (called a boucherie) once a month. Before the advent of electricity and freezers in our rural area – which happened when I was 14 years old – when you killed a pig, you would give a "voisin" (French for "neighbor"), a portion of pork, to each neighbor. When they butchered, <u>they</u> would return a similar cut and size.

When you had eaten fresh pork for a couple of days, the balance had to be salted down in crocks and left in the ensuing brine for preservation. The cured salt pork was used when boiling potatoes, snap beans and greens. Excellent!

Crushed corn fed the cows for beef and milk, cream, butter and cream cheese. It fed the ducks, geese, turkeys and chickens for fowl and for eggs. We even had a few sheep and goats from time to time. Later, during the war, we crushed the corn for cornbread and roasted some of it to mix in with coffee beans to stretch our precious rations.

Besides the crops of cotton, corn and soybeans, we grew the following: enough sugarcane for syrup and yellow sugar; melons and cantaloupe; field, black-eyed, and crowder peas; green and lima beans; beets, squash, okra, cucumbers, delicious Creole tomatoes, eggplant, carrots, spinach, shallots, cabbage, cushaw, garlic, onions, parsley, Irish and sweet potatoes and peanuts. No broccoli.

Our orchard offered peaches, plums, pears, pecans and walnuts.

So we had no money to speak of, but we were not poor. Our home was filled with love, cleanliness, discipline and spiritual nourishment. How did we cope? We bartered a lot. A grocery store on wheels – an old school bus refurbished with shelves in place of seats – came by once or twice a week. Mama would have a fryer or two in the coop and two or three dozen eggs to trade to "le garboteur" for his wares: soap, salt, needles, thread, canned meats and fish.

We fished and hunted to supplement our ample diet. My brother, Bobby, concocted a rabbit trap that was blessedly bountiful.

The war came and, for us – unlike our town friends – the plague of rationing was not too bad. Being so near the rice-growing, southwestern part of the state, one could buy a sack of rice – our staple choice – for pennies.

If corn was the "power" behind the farm, cotton was the cash crop but, in my estimation, it was also the scourge. Besides the fact that it so heavily relied on the right kind of weather, it required an inordinate amount of manual labor before the advent of machines, a development from which we never benefitted because my father – permanently scarred by the Depression – refused to borrow to buy "fancy machines."

In the spring, the soil had to be moist enough for the seed to germinate and push through. March and April winds could deprive the new plants of moisture during the formative weeks. Torrential rains could wash the seeds or young plants out of the ground. If the rain was right, the weeds loved it, too. Plowing and hoeing were required constantly. Boll weevils were waiting in ambush. Continuing through to the opening of the bolls in late August and throughout September, the magical makings for light, cool fabrics demanded unwavering attention and luck.

Picking the crop by hand was unadulterated misery. When a boll opens, the tips of the squares dry into sharp protrusions which destroy the thumbs and fingers without fail. Because you are trying to gather the crop before the dreaded hurricane season, you are in the field at daylight in heavy dripping dew; in five minutes you are wet to the bone which doesn't sound too bad for Louisiana at that time of the year. But it's cold before the sun matures. By 8:00 A.M., you're warming up. By 10:00, the rays are pumping the dew from your totally soaked clothes. Come lunch time, a child is smothering in five-foot tall plants. After lunch, it's back to the "salt mines" until dark.

Sol smiles as he pumps the perspiration from your clothing until he drains your diminished strength. Daddy used to have to hold us up over the tops of the stalks to let us catch a fresh breath.

This unrelenting slavery goes on for six days a week from about August 10th to early October...longer if the rains come, rains that mean money out of the family pocket, but rains that might mean a day off for your wracked body.

When Sally Fields played in a cotton-picking film, I told our children it was required viewing. For years they had been subjected to my tirades about the hardship of the cotton patch. Now they would see what modern slavery had been like. Cotton was one of the main reasons I liked school so much. It was a great incentive to leave home on the morning after high school graduation.

Besides all the hard work, I just couldn't seem to ever do things right. Read on...

TALE OF THE TAIL

And it comes to pass that in the third year of the reign of "Tiberius" Truman, word goes forth that the third son of the full crop of Pliny Tassin, being in the fifteenth year of his flowering youth, will henceforth be honored with the privilege of trimming the manes and tails of the mule and horse on the family farm.

Jim, a massive draft horse, is meek and agreeable; George, the white mule, is sprightly and self-centered, known to kick helpless piglets who insist on following him around to retrieve the few grains of undigested corn from his droppings.

In a remarkable fit of maturity, the son decides he will confront the most difficult challenge first. Bridling George and tying him to the fair sycamore in the barnyard center, he approaches the task with pride and apprehension, stroking the mule from the withers to the massive rump with authority and confidence.

George proceeds to be uncharacteristically accommodating, standing as stiffly as a canine on a fence post, afraid that one wrong move might mean a snip here or a snip there in the most sensitive places. Does George know the limpness of a long tail is not as accurate at swatting flies and mosquitoes as is a properly trimmed, medium-length swatter?

To himself, the son sayeth: "Hark, I must beware of the nub of the tail lest I draw blood and incur the wrath of the farm master."

George continues to stand rigidly like an equestrian statue in a military park, as if accepting this regular ritual as something to be endured.

So the third son feels upward from the fetlocks along the long strands of the tail until he reaches the nub, takes the large farm shears and whacks off the tail an inch or so below the knobby lump from which the fair appendage grows.

Lo and behold, a din of loud protestations echoes in the direction of the barn and increases in intensity so as to cause alarm and foreboding on the part of the fledgling groomsman.

It is the master! Himself!

White of face and booming of voice, he charges, "What the hell have you done to my mule?" Choking with disgust, he grabs the rope, unbridles the mule, and George happily charges off for greener pastures, no doubt relieved at being spared from witnessing the raging confrontation.

"Don't you know that a mule's tail should be trimmed by first removing the long outer strands until the shorter interior ones provide the desired and proper length?" he yells in white hot anger. Menacing with the rope, he demands, "Get out of my barnyard, this instant; this poor animal will have no defenses against the hordes of insects for months to come."

In the small washroom, with the door latched securely, third son looks into the small shaving mirror, trying unsuccessfully to hold back a torrent of embarrassing tears that must find release. In his heart he knows his father has just cause. The second son of the whole crop would have known better, because he watches, studies, learns.

It is perfectly clear that the third son knows nought about grooming mules' tails and has never been nor will ever be interested in learning.

The incident will henceforth serve as a favored conversation piece (initiated usually by the first and second sons of the whole crop) for all future holiday gatherings of the family.

George will be remembered as the beast of burden who goes about thumping his itchy thighs with an abbreviated tail for several months thereafter, probably wondering why he has lost control of his usually effective defenses.

And the son will leave the farm before daybreak on the morning after his high school graduation.

MAMA'S FLOWER GARDENS

For several years after we moved to our new house on OUR farm, our yard was barren. Chickens, ducks and turkeys clipped every blade of grass to augment their diet of corn with "salad." At some point, Mama talked Daddy into building fences perpendicularly to the side fences from the front corners of the house. Everything to the rear would be "fowl" territory and the front part would be flower gardens. It was not an easy sell with Daddy because at this time of slow emergence from the Depression, a farm to him was for food and sales; flower gardens were for the rich.

She was allowed her flower gardens, and flower they did. After the food was cooked, served, eaten and the dishes cleaned; after the clothes were washed, hung on the line, dried, ironed, and put away; after the figs, peaches, pears, plums, green beans, cucumber, pickles, cushaw rinds, tomatoes and corn and other assorted vegetables were peeled and cooked and preserved, Daddy and the boys spaded the soil, and Mama planted the seeds. She fertilized them with a rare mixture of chicken, cow and hog manure – mixed carefully with the rich sandy loam – hoed and pulled the weeds and cultivated the bountiful soil.

We had flower gardens that would have made Monet proud. Above a carpet of verbenas arose a pageantry including vieux garcons (bachelor buttons), a rainbow of roses, lilies, gladioli, poppies, tulips, touch-me-nots (which we touched too often, scattering seeds all over the wrong places) and daisies of multiple hues and shades.

Beside her family and her faith, this was her pride and joy and, although I hated the amount of work I had put into it, I, too, was proud of its majesty. I was dazzled by its uncommon beauty, intrigued by the giant moths and hummingbirds attracted to a feast of unlimited courses of nectar in a menu of seasonal entrees, fascinated by the wide variety of song birds chasing a cornucopia of juicy insects, worms and caterpillars in an eco-system of remarkable richness.

The farmer's wife was an artist of wide acclaim, one complimented lavishly by friends and relatives. While she was co-owner of our 40-acre farm with an acquiescing role in major decisions, la cour devant (front yard) was her personal queendom.

Where I grew up, it was the custom to have breakfast (dejeuner), dinner (diner), and supper (souper) – none of this lunch at noon and dinner at night. In the spring, summer and early fall, after supper, dish-washing and baths were completed, we sat and rocked on the porch and, as dusk and darkness arrived, the fragrances wafting up from the beds around us were almost overpowering, especially for a teenager with billions of hormones assaulting his helpless, developing body and romantically prone French genes.

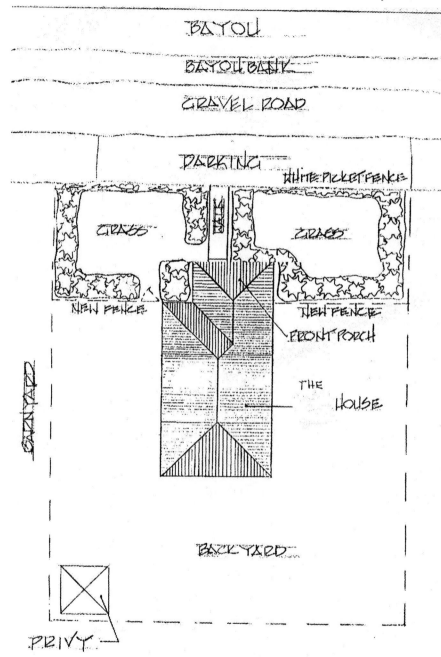

Layout of Mama's flower garden

PRIVATE/PUBLIC SCHOOL

There was no kindergarten when I was ready to begin school so I started in the first grade, and my first day of school was an eye opener. I spoke only French. My teacher, Miss Harris, spoke only English, making for a complicated situation when bodily functions had to be satisfied. To this day, I believe that the English-speaking teacher was assigned to that post to break the Creole kids of their "awful" French-speaking habit. Diversity was not encouraged in those days. English only – not even English first – was the order of the day at Cottonport Elementary.

Within a week, I could say, "Miss Harris, I need to go to the bathroom," instead of, "Miss Harris, il faut je va ca-ca."

While we are on the subject of school, I must use one of my "Why me, Lords." Cottonport school, including elementary and high school, was staffed with the finest teachers a student could want. From first grade thru twelfth, they were consistent: dedicated, well-educated, disciplinarians all, with personal attention given to each student. We were truly blessed.

I entered first grade around mid-September and loved every minute of it. On October 5th, my uncle showed up at the classroom telling Miss Harris that he had come to fetch my brother and me because Mama was very sick.

She had been bedridden for a week and looked awfully fat to me. She sobbed as we made our confusing good-byes and they wheeled her off to the ambulance to go to Lafayette, Louisiana, where she delivered a "blue baby," my baby brother, Sidney, who died at age 16 in a truck wreck. Sidney was the only child in the family of six children who was delivered in a hospital.

Some of the friends I made in the first grade are still friends today. I remember Myron Moreau, (yes, two Myrons in the same class) used to let me suck on his jaw breaker to help him get to the gum center. Now, that's friendship!

During this first year of school, the governor of Louisiana – true to his campaign promises – began offering "free" lunches to school children. I put "free" in quotes because, of course, they were not free; someone's taxes paid for them.

If you didn't like the food that was being served, you had the option to bring your lunch, usually toted in a paper sack or pail. Well, I had watched my mother making peanut butter or fig preserve sandwiches or chocolate sandwiches (cocoa, sugar, milk mixed into a paste), sometimes peanut butter and chocolate, for my brother's lunch for two years, and I wanted to enjoy the same fare when I enrolled. Heck with "free lunches." So I complained bitterly about the menu. The biscuits were too hard (and they were), the beans gave me gas (and they did), the Spanish rice was foreign to me (and it was). So for a while, Mama let me take my sandwiches to school.

The free lunch protesters met with their assorted cuisine under a large, ancient acorn tree. (That's what we called the live oaks on the school grounds). And believe it or not, you soon got tired of the same old sandwiches, even if they were chocolate sandwiches.

33

Invariably, people would begin trading sausage for chicken, boudin for cracklings, fig preserves for peach jelly, chocolate sandwiches for peanut butter and syrup, and so on. My cousin, Harvey Desselles, who was three years my senior, was an ace at trading up. But one day he met his match in the person of Pete à Callas (which means Pete whose father was Mr. Callas; I was Myron à Pliny).

Pete was the bad boy of the school grounds. He fought often and won so much that he could terrorize the whole student body. If fists didn't work, he scratched with his long dirty fingernails and bit with his uneven teeth. He was black and blue all over from defenders.

We were sitting around in a circle under a branch of the acorn tree one day when Harvey says, "Pete, what kind of 'samich' you got dere?"

And Pete replies, "Me, I got a geese 'samich'. What 'kine' you got, 'Harvaay'?"

"You want to trade; me I got chicken, Pete?"

Pete agrees to the deal and Harvey forks over his chicken étouffée sandwich on homemade bread to Pete á Callas and gets the "geese" sandwich in return. "Harvaay" should have known that it should have been identified as a goose sandwich, not a geese sandwich, but none of us were very big on English grammar. Harvey takes a big bite, chews a little, and comes charging up from his squatting position, yelling, "Dammit, Pete, that's not a geese 'samich', that's a grease 'samich'." Pete à Callas, with a smirk on his face, unexcitedly and not threatened in the least, replies, "Oh, dat's how you say dat."

Living on farms without rural electrification, farmers who slaughtered hogs in the winter would pack their sausage and crackling into crocks and cover the delicacies with the lard rendered from the pigs' fat backs. Sealed from the air, the cooked sausage and crackling would last for several months. As the meals and the lard were used, tiny fragments of meat would settle at the bottom of the crock. These lard drippings were what went into Pete's (I mean "Harvaay's") "geese" sandwich.

Twenty-nine years later I was invited to speak at a nine-state convention of the Public Relations Society of America. My subject was truth in advertising and publicity. The point of the talk was that if you begin telling less than the truth in advertising or publicity, your audience – as well as the media carrying your message – will soon cease to believe you. To make my point, I told the Pete à Callas story. The audience, many from redneck states like Tennessee, Arkansas, and Alabama, apparently liked my enhanced, if that's possible, Cajun accent. As I went on milking the story, I could tell I had them listening intently. When I delivered the punch line, "Oh, dat's how you say dat," the crowd roared. I soaked it all in and finished in Cajun English with: "Pete à Callas knew damn good and well how to say grease. And 'Harvaay', him, he never traded a chicken sandwich for a grease sandwich no more, I garontee you, cher."

Funny how things come around. A month after the talk, I took my family to the Piccadilly Cafeteria in Baton Rouge's Westmorland Village for dinner. As I came up to the counter to pay our bill, the children crowded around to get their chocolate mints. Opening my wallet, I handed my Bank AmeriCard to the uniformed cashier. She handed it back to me, saying the card was no longer accepted. The establishment was honoring the other card, MasterCard. I didn't have but a couple of dollars in my wallet. Shirley gave me that "don't look at me, I didn't bring my purse" look. The line of people waiting to pay their bills was beginning to stretch out for what seemed like several blocks. I could see myself washing dishes. Red-faced, the four children disappeared fleetingly through the door onto the sidewalk and walked briskly around the corner to the car. Their embarrassment reminded me of the times I would take a butcher knife and tomatoes from the garden whenever we went out for lunch at MacDonalds. Invariably, their faces were as red as the fresh, juicy Creole tomatoes.

Anyway, the Piccadilly cashier was apologetic but not very helpful. A voice way back in the line, appreciating my dilemma, yelled out, "I'll pay his bill." I looked over the millions of eyes fixed on my crimson visage and saw a nice looking 30-something fellow. He headed toward me at the front of the line.

"I'm sorry, I don't seem to remember you," my voice quavered.

He handed me his card and said, "Send me a check anytime. I heard you tell the geese sandwich story at the convention a few weeks ago."

I could have kissed the soles of his penny loafers. I didn't linger in the line that by now was snaking towards New Orleans. After shaking his hand briskly, I walked out into the warm, humid, early evening air that hovers over Baton Rouge from March 15th to Thanksgiving. It felt cool and light and dry that night.

When I got to the car, I could see the boys slinking down in their seats not wanting to be seen by the people leaving the restaurant. Only the tops of heads were showing. And there was Anne peering through the car window, afraid that her father would get hauled into debtors prison for failing to pay.

I swung the old VistaCruiser around and headed for home to write that check immediately.

"Second Grade"

Please excuse the long detour I took from first to second grade.

My second year teacher was Miss Loly Couvillion, a sweet spinster who, 12 years later, would be my classmate at Louisiana State University as she earned her masters degree.

When she read the class a story about a forester who would talk to the animals in his charge, I knew then that I would become a Ranger.

Twice a day, she would send one of her favorites to a grocery store across the street to purchase a Classic Coke. Looking back, I can sympathize with her needing a picker-upper to whip up her coterie of 24 snot-nosed charges in their quest for educational excellence.

Miss Loly could ritualize the act of drinking a Coke like she was partaking from the fountain of youth with a little Stoli mixed in. She would wrap a napkin around the bottle like it was made of blown glass from the world-famous Murano glassworks off the coast of Venice. We would watch in anticipation and envy as she took that first large swallow, smacked her lips and then, with hand over mouth, she would emit a muffled but resounding burp. By that age, I had never had Coke, only orange, strawberry and grape pop.

On my return with my precious cargo one day, I couldn't stand the temptation any longer. At the corner of the building, where she couldn't see me, I gave in and took a hefty gulp. The strong beverage stung my throat, fizzed through my nostrils, and I was still coughing when I handed her the "fix." Being inexperienced at chicanery, I didn't stop as I could have at the water fountain to restore the level of the precious elixir to its original mark.

She must have suspected, but if she noticed the diminished quantity, she didn't make an issue of it. Perhaps she knew she should not have been using one of her scholars as a runner for a bottle of pure power. But from that day forth, I was unceremoniously demoted from my position of the elect.

"Third Grade"

Monumental year. Teacher: Miss Narcille Lemoine, a pretty lady with doll-like features, who was dating our school principal, Mr. Lawrence H. Ducote. He would visit his future bride several times a day. By all appearances, it was a torrid romance, even in a nine-year-old's estimation. He was definitely infatuated with her. War came; he left. My sister's husband served with him on Leyte island in the Philippines where Mr. Ducote was a captain, I believe.

In late October of the third grade I almost died. One of my morning chores on the farm was to walk about a quarter of a mile along the road from our barnyard to a lane where the cows waited to be driven daily to our grazing pastures located at the back of our three-acre-wide by 13-acre-deep farm.

On that fateful morning, my father was leaving the barnyard in his wagon to deliver a load of soybean sacks to our next door neighbor, Mr. William "Slim" Morgan. I hitched a ride to the lane by holding on to the back of the wagon. It was fun dragging my feet in the loose gravel surface. The wagon wheels were rimmed with iron which made for loud crunching sounds.

Before we reached the lane, my father yelled that there was a car coming and not to cross. I didn't hear him.

Like it just happened a few seconds ago, I remember stepping out from behind the wagon and seeing the radiator of a car five feet away. Next thing I knew I was sitting up in the gravel. My father had thrown the reins to the horses, which proceeded to stampede down the road. Judging from the skid marks in the loose gravel, they later estimated that the young man who had run over me was going between 35 and 40 miles per hour. He jumped out of his car, Daddy picked me up in his arms, and we headed to town for a doctor. It was 6:00 in the morning. I remember praying because I thought I would die.

While my father held his profusely bleeding nine-year-old in his arms in front of the doctor's office – which was located in the rear of a pharmacy – Sims Tassin, a distant relative and the driver of the Model A Ford, went to get the doctor. When he returned with Dr. Kauffman, the chubby physician told Daddy that my severe head injuries required that I be stitched up without the benefit of a pain killer. I believe he thought I might go into a coma and never emerge. My knuckles, kneecaps and the tops of my feet were skinless. They had been dragged through jagged gravel before I popped out behind the car.

There were no broken limbs, only a broken head. My scalp had been torn off of one side and pulled back to the other, and I had a large dent on the left side of my head. My forehead was cracked from the hairline down to my eyebrows. From a mangled lower gum to the tip of my chin, the flesh was torn from the bone. I had several loose teeth and eventually lost one. Mine was a bloody, excruciatingly traumatized body, an open wound soiled with dirt, sand, gravel and most likely a bit of cow manure.

The pharmacist and Daddy held me down, promising always that it would take just a few more stitches, just a little bit longer. Three hours later we headed to the nearest clinic in Marksville, about 12 miles away, but stopped at home first to tell family members what had happened. They still didn't know.

When they brought me into the house, my mother and siblings smothered their sobs like ones I had heard at funerals. I knew it was bad by the size of their eyes. With scissors, they cut my little purple T-shirt down the middle and removed it. I could hear Daddy telling them in the kitchen that the doctor thought it was probably hopeless.

In clean pajamas, I was off to Marksville. I remember x-rays, a feeling of major stiffening, agonizing pain, crying parents who kept averting their stares. Fading in and out of consciousness. Hallucinations. Terrible thirst from loss of body fluids. Water not allowed; would cause brain to swell, they were told. After two days and nights of hanging between life and death, my father – who was convinced I wasn't going to make it anyway – gave me a gulp of Orange Crush. I plummeted into deep unconsciousness. They tell me my head swelled up to the width of my shoulders.

Three weeks later I came home. Two days after my return, pneumonia set in. Fever over 104 degrees Fahrenheit. I could barely stand to touch my boiling body with my hands.

Another three weeks later, still bandaged like a mummy, I was visiting my classmates. It was noon recess. One of my favorite friends of the female gender, Jackie Leary, saw me on the school grounds and fled bawling. Not too reassuring. Two more weeks and I was back in school, just two months total after the accident. Still bandaged around the head. Tightening teeth. Lots of homework. Life was sweet. Finished that year-of-years with A's and B's. Why me, Lord?

"Fourth Grade"

I was in Miss Maude Callegari's class, but I was not happy with the situation. I felt she was slow as molasses in January, in speech as well as in movement. I'm the son of Pliny Tassin; let's get moving. It was sheer agony. She knew all too well that I was unhappy, and I don't think she was too pleased with my attitude. One day she came into the class and announced that someone had to be transferred to the other fourth grade class taught by Miss Eloise Bordelon, a favorite of my older brother, Bobby. Anyway, Miss Maude said that they had pulled names out of a hat, and my name had been drawn, a miracle for sure. My heart (and my lungs and spleen and pancreas) leapt with joy, sheer joy. But I was already a public relations seedling clever enough to feign concern and doubt. Miss Eloise, who was at our 40th high

41

school reunion, was one of my favorites. Geography was big in her book and in mine, too. I knew there had to be a world beyond Avoyelles Parish, and I would confirm it later.

"Fifth Grade"

My teacher was Miss Alice Marchand, the strictest teacher I ever had. The diminutive lady could have stared down a 500-pound gorilla. The class had too many students for the space allowed; therefore, two rows of desks were banked together into one. Lucky me, Joan Thevenot and Nina Goudeau sat behind Clifton Jeansonne and me. We had a lot of fun cutting up when Miss Marchand was busy interrogating someone at the other side of the class.

"Sixth Grade"

Sixth grade found me in Miss Mary Ducote's class. The dean of all teachers was in her 60's then, I believe. She was dedicated and smart and challenging. While in the fourth grade, I had been sent by Miss Eloise to borrow one of Miss Mary's encyclopedias from her classroom across the hall. "Miss Mary, Miss Eloise would like to borrow your 'M' encyclopedia. We're studying about Maine."

"Okay, but first you have to spell 'encyclopedia', then you can have it." Spelling has always been a natural gift with me so I quickly rattled off the right answer. She asked the members of her sixth-grade class if anyone could spell the word and only a couple of girls owned up to the matter. With book in hand, I strutted out of her room like a Cajun at a fais do-do. She never forgot that incident so two years later I coasted through her class as a smiling teacher's pet.

I had a minor setback that year when I had an appendectomy. I still don't know if I really needed it, but it seemed that a rash of pupils required that same operation at the time, and they all seemed to be regarded as heros who had faced the brink of death when they returned. I remember having bad pains in the lower right abdomen, but the great volume of garlic and onions in the rich French diet we enjoyed at home could have been the culprits. Whatever, I remember being in the same room with Betty Ann Ducote, who was two years older and considered a high school wonder woman. The fact that my operation required only one single stitch has always made me wonder if the whole matter was strictly psychosomatic.

"Seventh Grade"

Miss Lucy Couvillion was our teacher. A very good one who beat the hell out of us with a thick paddle at the slightest provocation. Today, the Civil Liberties Union would pounce on her with a battery of liberal lawyers, but she taught us rightly that people had to be respected no matter what. Right, Pat?

One of my great friends, James Clyde Rosa, moved to Cottonport during that seventh grade year with his brother, Charles, and his elderly grandmother. His mother had died when he was five. Now, his father and uncle, both of whom had just been discharged from the service at the end of World War II, were gone, too, having been killed in an auto accident. The brothers were traveling along Highway 90, near Rosa, Louisiana, of all places, when an 18-wheeler crashed into their old car.

43

Clyde's uncle had recently been liberated from a German POW camp by a force which had included Clyde's father. Fate, fate, fate.

I suspect the boy's tumultuous youth had led him to books and the pursuit of knowledge as a panacea for a cruel and unreliable world. He was real, I mean real, smart.

We, who thought we were so brilliant, lost a lot of confidence when Clyde could expound intelligently on any subject. Finally, one day when he was reading aloud to the class about Marco Polo's travels, he went on to explain how the explorer's mission had sought to transport "species"– not spices – from the East. We all roared in relief to know that this wunderkind was human, and not some sort of perverted genius. His nickname became "Species."

"Eighth Grade"

Enrollment at Cottonport High was apparently booming to the point that the school had to send us to the band building located in the far corner of the campus, which must have measured a total of 100 acres. The school band was dormant at the time, and we used the band room for class. Mr. Clarence Chatelain, taskmaster of the old school, was our mentor. Each morning we could see him coming from the main cluster of buildings on the campus proper a half mile away. Until he arrived and during recess when he went to the lunchroom for coffee, we played and marched around with the instruments. It was a frolicking year.

"High School"

In ninth grade, our world changed from adolescence to who-knows-what as we began moving from classroom to classroom for different subjects. Teachers included Mr. Gaston Ducote, who taught English (he committed suicide years later, but I don't think it was our fault). His brother, Lawrence, had married Miss Narcille, my third grade teacher, and was now our principal and sometimes professor. Miss Frankie Cauillouet was a brilliant literature professor. A former religious brother and our principal (when Lawrence Ducote went off to war) was Mr. Gaston Dufour. He filled any position that was open from geometry to coaching. H. E. Dupuy taught us agriculture, an easy course for a farmer's son. He also taught us parliamentary law which has been a godsend in many situations since.

The most influential teacher in my case was Madeline Cassidy Ducote, just recently out of college. She taught English with an emphasis on theme writing, which she knew would be stressed for freshmen at the university. Being the consummate extrovert, I always strove to make my creations funny or shocking. One day she called me aside and suggested I might consider writing as a career. From small acorns do tall oaks grow. In a class of 33, I finished sixth or seventh, I believe, at graduation. But if I had taken Algebra II, I would have placed much farther down the line. Math was definitely not my cup of tea. Words – primitive, basic, funny, sad, descriptive, provocative – would become my friends.

Cottonport High didn't have a football team at the time, and I couldn't afford a tennis racket, but by the time I was a junior, I played first-string in basketball, softball and track. It's not easy when you're 5 foot 6¾ inches, dripping wet.

POST SCRIPT: In the spring of 2000, four Cottonport High classmates and wives got together in two beach condos in Destin, Florida, for a week-long mini-reunion. One night, after a salivating meal of grouper and lump crabmeat at Louisiana Lagniappe, we sat around and mused about our careers.

Here was Myron Moreau, former General Manager/Vice President of Production for Chevron Oil's Upstream Gulf Coast Unit. THAT'S BIG!

James Clyde "Species" Rosa, who retired from the Air force as an avionics electronics expert, was on a special team for the Inspector General which performed inspections on the inspectors. After retirement, General Dynamics attracted him as a logistics engineering specialist engaged in retrofitting F-16's. THAT'S LARGE!

Dick Juneau spent his whole career in the insurance field. When he retired from Financial Holding Corporation, headquartered in Kansas City, Missouri he was Corporate Secretary for every one of the conglomerate's 30 different companies. THAT'S HUGE!

How impressive and stimulating to be in the company of three old friends – all major achievers in industrial, military and business fields.

Cottonport High didn't give them their proven intelligence; that was God-given. However, Cottonport High provided the basis from which to educate and inform that intelligence and act upon it. And these are just three of the many achievers from that class.

Junior/Senior prom

Upper: Junior-Senior Prom, 1950. Does the Junior in the white shirt own a coat? Lower: Trying to look suave in an age when Hollywood glamorized smoking. Left to right: John Jeansonne, James Clyde "Species" Rosa, Aubrey Moreau, Buddy Normand, "Hot," Cecil Lemoine and Barton Ducote

THE GAMES CREOLES PLAYED

An old saying goes something like this: "All work and no play make Myron a dull boy." Almost.

As plastered in protest on previous pages, there was too much farm work to be done – especially for little children; however, this harsh memory does not obscure the sweet fact that we had barrels of fun during childhood.

You grandchildren are probably wondering – "without TV's, VCR's, DVD's and other alphabet soups – how in the world did you entertain yourselves?" Answer? Very well, thank you.

Just as our work load was beyond our years, so, too, were our "toys" and "games," which included boats and horses, swimming, diving, hunting, trapping, furnace-making, real rubber pistols, china berry guns, dangerous exploits, and parties (when we crossed that strange bridge into Girlsville).

Once we had convinced our parents we were proficient swimmers, we were turned loose on the bayou in front of our home to swim, boat, and fish.

Our swimming forms and techniques would have given today's school-trained "aquanauts" a big laugh. Yet we had amazing pleasure in and on the water.

Utilizing an old buggy spring, a half dozen neighborhood boys built a formidable diving catapult, anchored into the bayou bank a dozen feet above the water. When you ran and spiked the end of the board with both feet, the spring would come into play to help you break the bonds of gravity and hurl your fearless body six additional feet into the air for a grand total of 18.

Upon smashing the surface like a wounded cormorant, you swam underwater through branches, eddies, snags and sprigs for as far as you could get. Aided by a swift current, the object was to stay under and go farther than anyone else…to go until you could hear your heart throbbing in your squealing ears. The pinnacle of success was having your friends contemplating that you might have hit your head on a log and that your lifeless body was probably tethered helplessly on the muddy bottom. Mama never came to watch.

Some of us had old sodden, rotting, leaky wooden boats in which we would paddle upstream for a couple of miles and then drift back downstream to our point of origination, ramming frequently into each other's crafts and jousting with paddles and panache. We were Jean Lafitte's ragtag renegades!

In our early teens, Bobby and I saved up enough to order a Sears Roebuck rod and reel set, which we found quite efficacious in harvesting large-mouth bass. I worked hard at learning the technique, knowing that Daddy – a fish connoisseur of considerable credentials – would furlough the best angler from the field work in quest of supper.

Our trotline was most prolific, however, in food production. (Its name derives from trotting along the bank to see if something may be tugging on the branch to which the line is anchored.)

Time out: To the uninitiated, a trotline is a long primary trunk line with short, secondary bait lines attached to it at intervals.

When Mama killed a chicken for the pot, she kept the guts for bait, morsels of irresistible temptation and fascination to any respectable blue cat. For some reason – probably low pressure – rainy nights were especially rewarding. It was not uncommon in the morning to find seven or eight wiggling beauties dangling from a total of 10 hooks, in which case there would be joy, singing, and feasting in Tassinland that evening.

While brother Bobby was by far the best trapper of rabbits, I especially enjoyed making stick cages, setting their tender triggers with small ears of corn and waiting for hungry cardinals to take the bait.

I've heard it said that only in the human species is the female more attractive than the male, an adage so very true in the case of the lackluster grey and rust female cardinal when compared to the brilliant, vibrant, redder-than-fire male.

We'd keep them in a wire cage for a while until a sharp beak would take a hunk out of one of our fingers and then Mama would set the captives free.

As hunters, our main quarry was a red-breasted and grey-backed northern songbird which traveled south each winter where it would stop singing and provide us with tender bodies wrapped in fat from the abundant seed and grain of field and forest.

Particularly fond of holly and china berries – known to age and distill into a liqueur of considerable punch – the delicious darlings would stagger from branch to branch, gorging themselves on the "whiskey balls" until a major buzz would set in. Knock-kneed and cross-eyed, they would perch transfixed as if awaiting the mercy of cold lead. We would oblige.

I had my own horse, Frank, a Heinz 57 bag-of-bones scrub which could not have brought more pleasure and joy to me had he been a registered Arabian stallion from the king's stables. Even at 12 or 13, a horse gave one a measure of independence, mobility, and pride. Our galloping gang would meet at the bridge – less than a mile from home – and travel to parts unknown and unplanned.

Anyone with a horse to be broken could find a willing crowd of bronco busters, particularly in the early spring between tilling and planting. If a steed dethroned you, the soft dirt was a comforting safety mat. As the equine bucked and ran in the deep loose soil, fatigue would soon prevail, and he was easily subdued by the tag-team of riders. In 30 minutes, we'd have him pawing for mercy. You knew you had 'im when you could slide back to his rump and dig your feet into his flanks without being flipped over his head.

All of this was bareback, you understand. We were "Injuns." We were Cochise and his Apache braves.

On the face of the severely sloping bayou bank, stretching upwards to a plateau some 50 feet above the water's edge, was a network of cattle and kid trails. Although most were steeply inclined, some stretches ran laterally for short distances. From these level spots, we dug furnaces into the bank, punched chimney holes to stimulate draft, built fires in them with dried driftwood, and roasted sausages and pork chops. The victuals were fit for a king, especially one who might not mind rare pork.

In the fall and winter, from sunset to dark, swarming clouds of blackbirds traveled from their feeding grounds in the rice fields near Marksville to roost in the swamps of the Big Bend country beyond Moreauville.

A piece of pipe plugged at one end, a firecracker and a handful of gravel became an unreliable cannon. When we had no firecrackers, we used carbide, spat on the chemical and lit the escaping gas. We would detonate this marvel of modern weaponry and occasionally knock down a couple, which were promptly feathered, gutted, rinsed in the bayou, seasoned, and staked in the mouth of the furnace for dessert. You would have thought that these teenagers had bagged a couple of Canadian Ringnecks. This was living; we were big; we were smart. Providers, pioneers!

Bobby and I were almost teenagers before we saved enough money to order an $18.95 bike from Montgomery Ward. It was stiff and stingy with coasting, but it was ours. And it was red and white, much like the tricycle I had dreamed about and hoped Santa Clause would bring to me as a child. But didn't.

Instead of Evel Knievel, we neighborhood boys were more like the Evil Boll Weevils. We would line up a couple of truck tires on their sides and begin "cycle jumping" over them. When you failed, you fell out of competition. Another tire was added. Many wheels were bent, tires were deflated, chains were broken, but our trusty "Monkey Ward" two-wheeler rolled on like an old World War I tank.

Overly competitive, daring and unafraid, I suspect my propensity for hernias (three surgeries thus far) all began during those days of hammering the tires and my belly lining. What for? To fight the good fight. To test oneself. To win.

By now, you should have surmised that in several of our recreational endeavors, there was an element of danger, making the exercise so much more exciting: high diving, underwater endurance swimming in cloudy water through a myriad of obstacles, playing with fire, homemade cannon, boating battles, firearms, bronco-bustin' – to name a few.

Surely, you've heard of the Steeple Chase, but have you been exposed to the 'trestle chase'? Probably not, because in my day, it was a sport enjoyed – I would venture to estimate – by less than 10 per billion of the world's children.

Next to the latest railroad bridge over Bayou des Glaises stood – like a wooden Stonehenge – the skeletal remains of the previous structure, the pilings having been sawed off some six feet above the water. Picture rows of six-foot high, one-foot-in-diameter structural members standing five feet apart in staggering lines stretching 100 feet across the bayou.

The object of the competition was to leap from piling to piling without falling off and to reach the other bank first. To stop along the way for a breather or strategy planning was treacherous because of the speed and momentum in progress. Furthermore, restarting the process was like high-jumping from a standing position.

So what's so dangerous about falling six feet into the water when you know how to swim? If you fell, you ended up in deep driftwood – logs, branches, flotsam, and jetsam – accumulated along the old and new structures, forming a veritable Club Med for long, slithering water moccasins, basking in the summer's rays. The incentive to stay on was profound. I remember some of us, having lost speed or momentum or "guts," shinnying down a piling and jumping from log to log to reach the nearest bank in Olympic record time, impelled along by the thought of long, hot, sharp, poison-dripping fangs clamping down on your whatchamacallit.

Eventually Daddy dedicated an acre of precious land between our barnyard and the neighbor's property to a multi-use calf pasture, softball diamond and basketball court. Until then we played an assortment of low-capital-investment Creole games like "La Vieille Truie" (The Old Sow) and "La Plotte en Trou" (The Ball in the Hole).

La Vieille Truie was a combination of outdoor summer hockey and "Hit the Can."

Equipment: One stick per player; one can, preferably about 28 ounces; a two-foot-diameter circle scratched in the dirt to serve as base.

Draw straws for the order of players and to determine who will be "It."

One of the other players whacks the can with his stick, trying to hit it as far away from the base as possible. Whoever is "It" tries to knock it back to the circle, fighting a Siegfried Line of defensive swinging sticks, wounded shins, scrapes, cuts, and contusions, cow pies, horse manure, pig poop, and ca-ca de poule.

When he successfully maneuvers the can back to the circle, the number two player in the order gets to display his determination, bravery and intelligence deficiency. And so on.

"La Plotte en Trou" (The Ball in the Hole), a.k.a., "Holey, Moley, Rolley, Polley," required similar low-budget outlays: one soaking-wet tennis ball, one old rusty gravy spoon, used match sticks, a hog trough with fetid, murky water in which to soak the ball.

Number of players? Whatever.

With the spoon, dig a row of holes in a straight line, one hole per player, an inch apart, a third of a tennis ball deep.

Draw broken match sticks to establish hole assignments. Two players roll the ball back and forth over the holes until it drops into one.

The "holee" picks up the water-logged ball and tries to hit one of the scrambling players with the spinning, spitting sphere. If he succeeds, each player must run back and touch his hole with a foot and re-scamper while the new "hitter" returns to the base and seeks to splatter damage upon another prospect.

When a player misses, he earns a broken match stick in his hole. After three misses, he must remove his shirt and stand facing the wall of the barn and, if he's not a total nincompoop, bury his face in the wet stench of his armpit (for safety purposes).

From 10 paces away, the other players each get three shots at his bare back. If anyone misses altogether, the targeted player will have a similar opportunity on the "misser."

Sweet danger! Sharp pain! Exciting gamble! The thrill of victory and the agony of the feet…from running over dried corn cobs.

We were emphatically not pacifists; war was popular. Inner tube pistols and china berry guns were the weapons of choice. Played in and around our barn with its assortment of stables, corn cribs, hallways, full-story hay loft and accessible roofs, rubber gun conflicts offered much opportunity to blast opponents with a large strip of inner tube stretched from a clothes pin trigger (attached to the back of the stock) to the end of the barrel. Of course, we played shirtless.

Pop guns were made of elderberry, I believe, its limbs having a soft center which could be extracted with a haywire hook to transform the foot-long length into a barrel which would accommodate a china berry for ammo. A plunger was made of any type of wood that would swell quickly when wet.

A slightly over-sized projectile was carefully jammed midway into the chamber. A wad of spit on the frayed end of the plunger created an airtight pocket between its tip and the loaded berry. With a quick, forward thrust of the plunger, the berry would come whizzing out of the barrel, propelled by the compressed air between the plunger and the "bullet." The loud pop was a reality bonus.

When the berry found its mark on exposed flesh, one could expect an immediate, bulging, throbbing red welt – growing like the flower of retribution blooming in the target's belly.

While our brothers, uncles, cousins, teachers, and family friends fought in Europe and the Pacific, we fought our battles on Bayou des Glaises.

Although we could not have perceived it at the time, there were, in our games, answers sought and lessons taught about ourselves and others...lessons that were confidence instillers and character builders.

They taught us about honor, fair play, and teamwork and – like a flock of birds – the games established our place in the pecking order. I learned early on that it was much more fun being the "peck-er" than the "peck-ee." That fact may not be PC today, but it was as natural as a bee gathering pollen to make honey.

We swam, fished, hunted, trapped. We climbed trees to their smallest tallest branches, cooked out, jumped pilings, broke horses, conducted military campaigns, beat up "old sows" and each other with "Holey, Moley, Rolley, Polley."

We piddled, we paddled and we pedaled. We saddled, prattled and dawdled.

Simultaneously, our lives were becoming addled, muddled and befuddled. Were we still children or something else? And then something strange happened.

Boats and BB guns, makeshift cannon, wild horses and cooking furnaces, catching fish and trapping birds, bikes that wouldn't coast – all of these, and more, lost their attraction.

Our voices began to crack like asthmatic bullfrogs. Our upper lips, legs, the whole body seemed to be hairing up. Chests were sore. Perspiration became malodorous and notable to all bystanders.

And girls who had been nowhere were...**E V E R Y W H E R E**!!

The opposite gender had always been of interest to me, but this was different. I could hardly have been more fascinated had the sun come up in the west, if clocks had moved counterclockwise and toilet water had flushed clockwise, if fish had had feathers and birds, scales.

We polished our shoes and wore them, combed our hair with Brilliantine, brushed our teeth without having been told to do so; even kept our fingernails clean. What was going on?

My horse, Frank, was not nearly as beautiful. Our bike still didn't coast worth a darn, but who cared?

I went to a party at Larry Armand's house. We played post office, and I was introduced to legalized kissing. My face was glowing and as hot as if I had been standing in front of a blazing bayou-bank furnace. My heart was coasting. It was much more fun than being bucked off into field dirt. These creatures smelled sweeter than Mama's flower gardens; their lips were redder than the reddest male cardinal, and they had much better legs.

I had contemplated the priesthood.

I would reconsider.

SELF-ESTEEM: WHAT'S IN A NICKNAME?

An uncle by marriage on Daddy's side was named Wilmore Desselles. His nickname was "Bool" but I believe it was really "Bull," mispronounced by his French-speaking friends and family. No doubt, "Bool" was full of "bull," and I loved him dearly. Not coincidentally, he appeared to like me a lot, too.

Handicapped since childhood, "Bool" had a severely twisted foot and ankle and walked with a terrible limp on the outside of his wretched foot. To me, he was tall and straight and handsome with a laugh so infectious your belly would ache.

"Bool" thought I was the proverbial "cat's meow" and his constant reinforcement raised the level of my self-esteem to a point approaching, if not surpassing, egotism. His son, Harvey, was the same type of happy-go-lucky person who felt the same way about me and vice-versa.

At the same time, my sister, Helen, was always telling me how great I was (see Dedication).

One weekend, one of Harvey's relatives, a boy named Pete, came to visit and brought along a set of boxing gloves. Under a pecan tree in the barnyard we all went a few rounds with each other and, being fearless, I did pretty well considering I was the smallest of the lot. When I polished off a boy two years my senior and a dozen pounds heavier, "Bool" beamed and pronounced, "Boy, you're a 'hot shot.'"

From that day forth, Hot Shot became my nickname. The "shot" was later dropped but to almost everyone at school, even including some of my teachers, I was known as "Hot." Can you imagine what that can do for your feelings about yourself? It made me strive to do better – in sports, academics, and leadership.

After we were married, Shirley thought it was time to drop the "Hot," not so much because my ego was running wild with itself (although looking back, it often did), but because I believe she felt it held double entendres.

After I've had a couple of glasses of wine, and some of my old friends ask why I've dropped the "Hot," I tell them that at one point Shirley said, "I know you're hot; you know you're hot, but do we have to tell everybody?"

It was a lonely feeling no longer having that crutch, that super-positive nickname; however, when Jimmy Carter became president and allowed that "Hot Shot" was his nickname, I felt much better not owning up to my old sobriquet (guess what my political persuasion is). But my nickname was good while it lasted, and I often wonder what growing up would have been like without "Bool" as an uncle and Helen as a sister. Why me, Lord?

What would it have been like if my nickname had been "ca-ca" or "stupo" or "foo foo" (crazy) or "coo coo" (crazier) or "poo poo" (messier)?

Which leads me to one of my favorite Cajun jokes about Poo Poo Boudreaux, who hated his name so much he went to the courthouse and had it legally changed. He was tired of everyone teasing him and making fun of his handle.

When he left the seat of government whistling and smiling, a passerby asked, "What's the matter with you, Poo Poo Boudreaux; you're usually frowning and fussing?"

Proudly, he responded, "Don't call me Poo Poo Boudreaux nomore; I've just had my name changed."

"What is it now?"

"It's Poo Poo Landry!"

(Oh well, I was sure you had heard it, too.)

Anyway, I would need all the self-esteem I could find for the cold world facing me on leaving high school.

GOING AWAY...AND STAYING

[Author's Note: Attention Grandchildren – The information which follows is not included for its shock value. Rather, it seeks to illustrate how bad decisions can follow you around for a lifetime.]

On the moonlit bayou to the right of the gravel road, fog lifts lazily to reveal a few snow white egrets feeding along the water's edge. It's just 5:00 A.M., the morning after my high school graduation, and Daddy is driving me to Mansura to catch the 5:30 train to Baton Rouge. Talk about not letting grass grow under your feet.

As we hit the minor dip under the railroad trestle, my insides protest with pronounced vehemence; last night I graduated from high school, but I misbehaved shamefully.

In one way, I was regretting having to leave best friends of both genders, not to mention a stalwart supportive family. I was also trying to act grown-up when I drank everything from gin to vodka, wine and beer, bourbon and, yes, creme de menthe from the neighboring tables at the dance held at the Blue Moon Club in Bunkie. Jerk!

But now, I have to go. My head feels like it's been run over again by a Model A Ford; my stomach – filled by a loving but crafty mother with sausage, eggs, grits, biscuits, fig preserves and milk – would prefer to be on a three-day fast.

You see, for the first time, I came home drunk last night. Not tipsy, not inebriated, not under the influence or any other softer sounding terms. I came home drunk and – on the morning after– I am deeply remorseful like any other sobering drunk. Disgusting!

Got home at 3:00 A.M., staggered around the front yard as my transportation sped away (at least I didn't drive). When I fell, my brother, Bobby, hauled me in as my ashen-faced, saintly mother held the door. I will never live at this wonderful home again, and this is the way I choose to depart. Stupid!

As Daddy chugs along, bobbing and weaving in our 15-year-old '36 Chevy, with its knee-action spring system long shot to hell, I am thankful that he keeps quiet.

Wish I could have another chance, but no way. I know I've lost face for all time. The eggs and sausage are now chasing the grits and biscuits.

We soon reach the end of the gravel road which intersects with the blacktop to Moreauville to the right and Mansura to the left. On the corner is a small grocery store/barroom where I've watched too many bourré games. It has a separate room for the Negroes to dance and drink, placing their orders through a small window. In large neon lights, I see a sign reading "Dixie Beer."

Oh nooo! I must open the window, but I'm on the side with the missing handle. I slip quickly over the front seat to the back and open up to fresh morning air. Hanging my head out, I look down and realize I can't stand to see the ground racing by. Imbecile!

My pretty good reputation with family, friends and school all blown to bits.

Pliny knows I'm suffering the worst self-inflicted retribution; he plays like he doesn't realize I've jumped into the back seat, that I'm still woozy, that my breath is as sour as week-old dishwater, that my eyes are hemorrhaging.

We're driving by my Uncle Bool's house. The lights are already on. He suffers terribly with his handicapped leg and foot. I think of all the good times we've had there especially during muscadine season. He's the one who nicknamed me "Hot Shot." Remember?

Looking for deliverance, I reason that my friends will meet me at the train station and support me in my time of agony. If I can just make it to the restroom at the depot.

Soon we'll be on our way to Baton Rouge to attend the annual Future Farmers of America Confab on the Louisiana State University campus.

If there's any redemption on this inauspicious morning, it is in knowing I will not, if God permits, ever be a farmer. I've been an active farmer's son – not a good one, mind you – for a dozen years and that's long enough. After several years of hurricanes followed by drought, my father originated one of the most clever sayings I have ever heard: "Don't become a farmer, son, because it always rains in your wallet."

My wallet is flat because I've been a farmer's son, but I'll have a free room under Tiger Stadium for a week during which time, I will get a job, save some bucks and plan to start the University next year. Simple!

We drive by the "We Go Inn" and "Leo's Bar and Lounge" where I've spent too many of my nights in the last two years. More neon signs: "Pabst Blue Ribbon," "Regal Beer," "Budweiser." H - E - L - P!

Like cotton-mouth moccasins, my friends are all at the station, looking as unsteady as I am. Daddy helps me with the used paper bag filled with assorted sandwiches as well as my brown, scarred cardboard suitcase, the kind with the two fake leather straps running vertically from the unraveling handle. The straps go nowhere – perhaps a sign of my life to come.

No time for the restroom; the train's a-coming. We can hear it approaching. I purchase my ticket just as it comes into the station, hug my Daddy, hop aboard (more like struggle aboard), and we begin pulling out.

Daddy smiles and waves. I'll never forget that smile. Did it say, "Good riddance?" I was a lousy farmer's son, always wanting to be somewhere else, with friends of both gender; practicing and competing in sports; raising hell that was tame compared to today's antics. Is Daddy laughing at me, knowing that my pain is the best medicine I can swallow on my way out? Is it a practical smile that knows he will have one less mouth to feed?

For the 75-odd miles to Baton Rouge, there is never a time without a long line to the restroom in our car, filled mostly with pale-faced, trembling graduates.

When we go over the Mississippi River Bridge, I feel my stomach squeezing up into a stone-tight knot in a spot in the general vicinity of my esophagus. My temples are serving as retaining walls for my pounding brain.

Heading down the other side of the structure, I lose the good fight. Thankfully, my mother's brilliant breakfast doesn't make it to LSU.

Three hours later, I have registered for the convention, found my bunk in the stadium, showered severely as if to wash away the sins, dressed in my only other suit of clothes and I'm in Christ the King Chapel on campus for late Sunday Mass.

By now, my surroundings are coming into focus as I ask for His forgiveness and pray for willpower to mend my wicked life. I am definitely penitent.

Four blocks away lives the girl of my dreams, who may well be at this very same Mass.

Could she be that cute young thing sitting on the aisle just a few pews ahead of me? Naw. She doesn't look a day over 16. Absolutely too young for a "man" of 18.

Two-and-a-half years later, we will walk down this same aisle.

Monday morning, I catch the downtown bus to the state capitol and go to the Secretary of State's office on the 15th floor. The secretary is Mr. Wade O. Martin, Jr. Surely, I reason, with a name like Martin, he will have a job for a Creole like Tassin. Nothing (although a year later, he will have a job for my older brother who will work for the state for 31 years until retirement).

Then I go to the State Department of Education, a couple of floors above, I believe. "What can you do?" the school-marm type asks over her wire spectacles.

"I can type 55 words a minute," I respond proudly. Meanwhile, the young lady at the desk next to my inquisitor is humming away at 90 words a minute, minimum, no pauses for erasures; no job for me, either.

On Tuesday, I go to see a native from Cottonport who has a well-known reputation for generosity in helping back-home people find jobs. Maxie Hollis, a physically handicapped but mentally brilliant and spiritual super-gentlemen takes me to see the assistant director of the Louisiana Department of Revenue in the Capitol Annex. Mr. Curtis Breaux speaks to me in French, to begin with, putting me at ease. "Comment ça va?"

"Bien, merci, Monsieur Breaux." I explain I am hoping to go to the University someday, but there is simply no money at this time.

"Have you ever picked cotton?" In disbelief I wonder, "Does it show?"

"Yes, since I reached 6 years old."

"Does your father know Dr. "Babs" DeNux, the legislator from Marksville?"

"Yes." I was sure he did, at least vaguely.

"Go home and get a letter of recommendation from the good doctor and then report back here next Monday. If the letter is favorable, you've got a job as a stockroom clerk which involves heavy lifting; that's why I asked you about picking cotton. Can you live on $150 a month?" he concludes. What? A cool $150 a month, $1,800 a year? During the year after my auto accident, our family lived on $67 for a whole year.

"Yes, Sir!!"

With Maxie, I walk down the cool air-conditioned, marble-walled hall to his office in the auditing division. No dew, no battering sun, no caterpillars, no boll weevils and yet it's my experience as a hard-working cottonpicker that has landed me my first real job. Why me, Lord?

I hitchhike home and on Saturday morning Daddy takes me to the courthouse where Dr. DeNux meets his constituents weekly. The man, a prominent physician, interviews me, sits down at an old Royal typewriter and personally types my letter which in essence tells Mr. Breaux that my parents are supporters of his and the Earl K. Long administration.

Now, how to find the money to live on for the next two weeks before I get my first check. I recall a senior field trip with my agriculture teacher and an influential local businessman, pharmacist Gano Lemoine, who asked me about my future plans and indicated he might be able to offer financial assistance (loans, I assumed). So here I am later that Saturday morning telling him of my plans and possibilities. "How much do you need?" he asks.

"Thirty dollars."

He rings out the cash register and pulls out three tens, which I will pay back 15 days later.

Hitchhiking was easy in those days. I'm back in Baton Rouge before noon Monday, turn in my letter, and later find a room in a boarding house. Soon I will be in Mrs. Landon's apartment house where Maxie lives with his sister, Catherine, and Mary Ann Gagnard, also from Cottonport. It's like one big happy family. Lots of bourré games, at least one home-cooked meal a week at Maxie's and Catherine's table, financed by the Hollises who are generous beyond words and well established in high-paying jobs.

In a few months, brother Bobby leaves his job with the Avoyelles telephone company and joins me. Then I convince one of my best classmate friends, Aubrey Moreau, to come aboard and the three of us move into a larger apartment on the second floor of the Landon house, a modest but more than adequate unpainted structure.

In retrospect, the year between high school and college studies is a blessing, giving me a chance to cleanse myself of a few more wild antics left in my system.

Money is good. Lots of state holidays. Good working conditions. From the topmost sixth floor, we pick up mail and process it. We haul all supplies, truckloads of 'em, from the basement to the sixth floor and then dispense them to the three floors below. As government would have it, there is no elevator from the fifth to the sixth level. Sounds like a major snafu, but I don't care. It is clean and cool.

On my first day at work, a gigantic truck filled with cases of envelopes has to be unloaded and its contents hauled upstairs. It's a snap. In the stockroom, there are large bins from the floor to the ceiling, which must be 20 feet high, where the envelope cases, each containing a dozen or so smaller boxes, have to be stacked. A large ladder on skates, such as ones you saw in the old shoe stores, rolled back and forth.

My immediate supervisors, Sam Alysce and Joe Purpera, come to check my work and ask why I am struggling with the boxes as I climb up the ladder to put them into the top bins, especially since many of the lower bins are empty.

"Well, it says right on the case here, stack this waaaay up."

Actually it reads, "stack, this way up," having something to do with keeping the weight and pressure off of the gummed envelope flaps to deter them from sticking together in the heavy Louisiana humidity.

Sam and Joe laugh their heads off at this country bumpkin, but they like me from that day on.

In the 50 years since, I have told that story many times, endearing me to people who seem to empathize with this green naive country bumpkin who probably falls off the turnip truck daily. Everybody likes a fool, they say, and me, I "shore" have my share of "admirers."

In those patronage days, you were expected to do other chores beside your regular work...like having to go to the Governor's mansion to stuff campaign envelopes, driving a sound truck on weekends but – you guessed it – it was as easy as catching catfish on a rainy night on a trotline baited with chicken guts.

While Joe Purpera and Sam Alysce were the work bosses of the stockroom, there was also a political boss who came to work late, took long lunches, left early, read his racing forms and listened to baseball games on which he invariably placed bets.

In fact, one of my duties was to take his bets to a bookie joint on Lafayette Street in downtown Baton Rouge. By phone, he would arrange for the "lookout" to be waiting for me. Inside the second floor "office" was a huge circular counter with a bank of telephones manned by grisly-looking Damon Runyon types – who all had cigarettes hanging from the corner of their wet lips and short-brimmed hats on the back of their unkempt heads – just like the movies.

The roll of his bills was enveloped in a strip of paper with instructions on which horse, which race, which game, point spread – all arranged by phone but confirmed thereon. I always felt a kind of dirtiness mixed with exciting danger when I returned to the Annex.

I didn't want to be a "runner" for the rest of my life, and looked forward to getting an education.

One of the other employees was a high school summer worker who would soon introduce me to Miss Right!

One year to the week after I began my Revenue job, I entered LSU summer school. Revenue Administrator Loftin later allowed me to keep a part-time job in charge of records and tax returns in a large quonset building behind the Annex. (Catherine put in a good word for me.) When someone was being audited, I had to produce the records. It involved intermittent work, which facilitated studying during the slow periods.

To qualify as a part-time employee, I had to work less than 40 hours a week, so Mr. Loftin let me work 39. On Saturdays, I sold shoes at Myron's Shoestore and later at Baker's. On Monday nights and one weekend a month, I attended National Guard drills and received compensation there, too. I worked as a custodian of the gym

71

armory and got a free room in the gym. All in all, I was saving money. By the time I was a sophomore, I was married; a year-and-a-half after that we had a child, and my duties expanded to include the required free service on the LSU school newspaper staff. When Mike came, chief cook and bottle washer duties were added to a schedule that had me feeling like a warmed over mummy. How was I doing in school? Average I thought, but I was so busy, there was little camaraderie between me and my classmates, many of whom were as busy outside school as I was.

COLLEGE DAZE

For me, LSU was not a time for fun and games; I had let les bon temps roulez during that year between high school and college.

In freshman summer school, I made all B's. From then on, I made lots of A's, some B's, and an occasional C plus one D in philosophy. The prof for the latter course had a nerve-wracking tic, laughing vigorously after every sentence, no matter how serious its content. I sat there emotionally drained and pining for the next period. To be honest, I must not use that as an excuse for my poor performance. As a quasi-artistic type, I simply am not a logical person and logic was heavily emphasized. I did not repeat the course because I didn't think I could have done any better.

With a D, I considered my grade-point average mediocre. Imagine then my shock when I was notified by the dean that I had placed first in my Journalism graduating class and would be honored with both national journalism fraternity (Sigma Delta Chi) awards – one for the highest grade point average and the other from the faculty, students and professional members for "Character, Scholarship and Competence to Perform Journalistic Tasks as the Outstanding Male Graduate in Journalism."

Whew! More rewarding than stacking boxes waaay up.

So busy had I been with three jobs, my National Guard service, a wife and a son and another on the way, I had not had the luxury of "chewing the fat" and partying with my classmates where I might have gauged how well or poorly I was doing, scholastically speaking.

At the end of my junior year, I left the Department of Revenue for a full-time writing job.

I still needed a full year to graduate, a challenge I would surmount with night school and correspondence courses. In spite of that disruption of schedule, I would earn my degree in four years. All in all, it was still a breeze compared to picking cotton.

Citation
for Achievement
Sigma Delta Chi
Professional Journalistic Fraternity

Myron Jude Cassin

having been nominated by an authorized committee composed of student, faculty and professional members, is hereby cited because of his general excellence in

Character, Scholarship and Competence to Perform Journalistic Tasks

as the Outstanding Male Graduate in Journalism

at   Louisiana State University

in   January, 1956

_____
NATIONAL PRESIDENT

_____
NATIONAL SECRETARY

Journalism award

75

"caREAR" IN GEAR

In 1955, Journalism Professor James Price came into class one morning to announce that the United Givers Fund (now United Way Campaign) was looking for applicants for public relations director. Not knowing what public relations really meant, I applied as did eight other candidates, mostly from radio and TV stations, who did know.

They didn't ask me if I had ever picked cotton, but I got the job anyway. This was one of those lucky forks in the road that can affect the rest of your life, and it did.

My new boss, Myron Falk, (Myron's Shoestore, Myron Falk, Myron Moreau, Myron Tassin: what gives?) was pleasant, a great leader, knowledgeable and industrious. To his dying day, at 90-plus, he was my good friend.

For someone who didn't know what public relations entailed, I was soon immersed in writing for radio, TV, newspapers, magazines, brochures, billboards, films, speaking to community groups and learning about the various strata that make a community tick. And my salary jumped from $250 to $350 a month.

We traded in our old faded maroon Olds for a 1952 Ford Crestline with a continental kit on the trunk. Why me, Lord?

A couple of weeks later, my parking brake failed, it rolled backwards down the steep driveway at the office and smashed into a tree across the street. Adieu continental kit. Why me, Lord?

Working at UGF was a dream until 1958, when I exceeded the budget for the position, and left to open a one-man public relations and advertising office of my own. Within a few weeks, I had signed up a Ford dealer, a camera house, a shopping center and a black perpetual care cemetery. Look out, gray flannel suit!

In 1960, attorney Alvin Rubin, who would later become a federal judge in New Orleans and who served as perpetual secretary-treasurer of the United Givers Fund, called to ask if I might be interested in closing my office and becoming executive director of the Louisiana Architects Association (the American Institute of Architects in Louisiana). I was interested; I was interviewed; I was hired, and I sold my business.

It was a pleasant, challenging and rewarding experience working for so many talented, frustrated and temperamental artists.

Although I loved my job, it was a real stressful position, as magazine editor, insurance plan administrator, legislative lobbyist and organizer.

Once, when we opposed certain political forces, my rear windshield was shot out one night. The next day, when I turned the key to start my car, a large cloud of smoke bellowed in front of the blue Chevy. Out in a flash, I ran from the car to see a big black switching locomotive on the tracks a few feet away. Paranoia can be powerfully suggestive.

In 1966 my friend and next door neighbor Gary Taylor, district manager of the Zenith television distributor for parts of Louisiana and Mississippi, said he was being elevated to director of the whole Zenith division and wanted to know if I was interested in replacing him. It seemed to be a pretty simple job. Gary went to work late, came home early and had long leisurely lunches with Penny in between. He promised me I would increase my income by 50 percent.

My recommended replacement at the LAA was Dick Thevenot of Cottonport, with whom I had ridden "The Flash's" school bus for too many years. An LSU journalism graduate, too, he had followed me in the UGF job and is still at the LAA position 34 years later.

I took the job with the Zenith Distributor, increased my income by 50 percent that first year, just as my good friend and fine boss, Gary, had promised. I also left at the end of those 12 months with a stomach ulcer.

As a self starter, I did not fit in with the pressure of a sales organization. Quotas, contests, shrinking territories and MEETINGS, MEETINGS, MEETINGS – mostly to stimulate action from the unmotivated – were not my cup of tea. But they taught me how to sell, which comes in handy in any work.

In the charming two-story "slave quarters" of the historic Warden's House in Baton Rouge, I opened Tassin Publishing. Although medical science tells us now that ulcers are not caused by stress, mine went away in six weeks just the same, never more to return. Our income dropped by half, but we were happy again. In one year, it would double; in three, triple.

In two years, my new partner and I were editing and publishing eight or nine professional and trade journals, from architects to engineers, realtors and municipalities to cattlemen and savings and loans...even the national AIA's student "magapaper." We handled local and state political advertising campaigns and did PR for a prominent architectural-engineering firm.

Four years later, I became a consultant for one client three days a week in New Orleans, and sold my 75 percent interest in the business to my partner. Extensive travel – domestic and foreign – was fun at first but after four years I realized that I wasn't noticing when the plane had taken off or landed; it was time to go. Then, too, the call of the land, which I had resisted as an adult and pooh-poohed as a child, was getting louder.

Perhaps, I could invest in acreage, manage the properties and write books as well.

Celebratory kiss on climbing – with John and Carol Stroop – to the
peak of 12,000+ foot Mount Crested Butte.

<u>LAND HO!</u>

In 1966, we had just settled into our new home on Hyacinth Avenue in Baton Rouge. Designed by Ross Murrell, architect, our house was divided into three major components: the children's end, our master bedroom on the opposite end and community property in between.

Soon, Shirley and I developed a relaxing routine of meeting in the sitting area of our new bedroom on Sunday evenings to discuss any issues at hand such as the children and their needs, work and its pressures, financial matters.

One fateful Sunday night, we talked philosophically about what we hoped to be doing economically in the years ahead. Thankfully, long standing bills and debts were being retired with dispatch; our savings were slowly beginning to mount.

As much as I had disliked farm work, some of my happiest leisure hours now were being spent in the garden in our side yard. There was something therapeutic, spiritual, to tend a small seed into a plant and its fruit to the family table. Without hesitation, we agreed that land would surely be a good investment.

Within a month we had purchased six acres at the corner of Old Perkins and Bluff Roads, some 12 miles from our house. Price: $6,000. On weekends, the whole family worked to improve the place. We cut away the prickly briars under the trees, trimmed off branches up to six feet, piled up dead wood and dragged it into the ravines to stymie erosion.

Two years later, we sold the parcel to a Baton Rouge lawyer for $12,000 and with it purchased 12 contiguous acres on Bluff Road, went through the same routine, sold part of it to the Highway Department for Interstate 10 access and the rest to a Baton Rouge engineering company. We used the proceeds for 18 acres farther on down Bluff Road, proceeds from which purchased 80 acres across the road from Asphodel Plantation in East Feliciana Parish. It sold for $60,000 three years later.

The $60,000 was used as a down payment on 1,168-acre Cliffwood Plantation in West Feliciana Parish. During a six-month purchase agreement period, I was able to sell half of the acreage at almost twice my purchase price, leaving me with over 500 acres virtually free.

Before purchasing 1,200-acre Little Badger Ranch in Central Colorado in 1978, we executed three other similarly successful ventures. Although individually not as large as Cliffwood, we worked to improve each property before reselling. Some of the parcels were agricultural; most were recreational. In Colorado, we would eventually acquire some 6,000 more acres.

It was easy to foolishly begin thinking that Hot Shot was Hot Stuff.

When inflation began exploding, however, I quickly came to realize that almost no matter what land you bought during these double-digit-inflation ("Hot Shot" Jimmy Carter) years, it was bound to super-inflate as people sought to put their money into something solid like land. I wasn't smart; I was lucky beyond words to be in the right ventures at the right time.

Do you believe in crossroads? In forks in the road where one is right and the other wrong? I don't. I believe that oftentimes, either fork can be made to work.

I believe some people never take risks because they're afraid to make mistakes. Many are concerned about what people – parents, siblings, friends, associates – will say "if I fail." If you can get over the fear of failure, you've taken the first giant step to success.

Of course, preparation, research and due diligence can all reduce risks. My first question in buying property is, "Can I get my money back?" Secondly, if I can't sell it at a profit, do I like it sufficiently (and can I afford) to keep it for a long time?

By 1979, when we moved to Colorado, almost all of the Louisiana land was sold, the proceeds from which would be used to continue the process. From that time on, I was hooked.

As of this writing, we are reducing inventory, with a total of just under 350 acres remaining. At age 69, it's time to simplify.

THE VAGABONDS

We have friends and family who have lived in the same house for 30 or more years. Thank God for these solid, steady people whose stability works to balance the frequency of moves with those of us who were born with wanderlust.

In the 48 years since our marriage, we have lived in 25 places: nine in Baton Rouge, one in Waveland, Mississippi; back to Baton Rouge where we repurchased the house we had sold on moving to Mississippi; three in Colorado Springs, Colorado; two near Cotopaxi, Colorado; four at Westcliffe, Colorado; three in Shalimar, Florida; one in Destin, Florida; two in Crested Butte, Colorado.

No, we're not career military people. Yes, we've always paid our rent. But there are reasons why we have moved so much.

Since I began writing books in 1968, several of these moves were precipitated by various publishing projects; plus, since our entry into land investments, we have often bought a place, renovated it and lived in it before resale.

Other moves were stimulated by a strong desire to experience different types of living, i.e. the city, the mountains, the forest, the bay, the beach and two country clubs. I don't play golf, but I believe some of the most beautiful, improved land in America is in its golf courses.

I am not interested in living in the desert or on the plains. I've been on maneuvers in the New Mexico desert, and I don't miss the varmints, reptiles, insects and extreme hot and cold temperatures. I've already lived in the flat Mississippi River Delta, which is basically the Louisiana plains.

Our biannual moves, on average, have been exciting, enjoyable, and rewarding. They've also been hard, but I liken the distress of a move to a bad cold: it lasts a couple of weeks, and then you feel much better.

We truly admire people like the Pete Lavergnes, Amar Lancons, Bobby and Joseph Tassins, J. T. and Neff Lynn Hills, Buddy Normands, Vernon Bahlingers, Billy Dragos, Doug Harpers and Murff O'Neals, who lived in the same house for decades...some approaching a half century.

I must admit I was thinking just this past summer that my appetite for adventure is waning. Two days later, we toured a site on a high bluff – a modest cliff, if you will – overlooking a crystal-clear, gushing, salmon-infested river, banked by verdant wetlands and with a view of 13,000-foot Paradise Divide little more than a dozen miles away. Had to step on my heart. Who knows?

"Colorado via Alaska"

There are sound reasons for two major moves out of state. First, we went to Bay St. Louis-Waveland, Mississippi, so I would be nearer my consulting work in New Orleans, without having to live with our children in what I considered to be a mid-70's urban jungle.

We moved to Colorado because of Alaska. Strange, but true.

In 1968, I went to Alaska to produce a travel brochure for a lodge owned by a friend. It was about 35 miles over the mountains from Juneau...beauty unsurpassed, wildlife in great proliferation, grandeur that captured your inner being and self-reliant people who made you ashamed of your pampered life – all of these stimuli worked on my psyche to a point that I came back to Baton Rouge in a mesmerized state. I could not stop thinking about it all. One day on the back porch swing, Shirley said, "Either you've got to take us there or you have to shut up about it." I knew she was serious because she seldom speaks so sharply.

As part of my compensation on the project, the owners of the lodge had guaranteed a couple of weeks gratis for me and my family if I could get us back at my expense.

Five months later, after borrowing from the cash values of an insurance policy we had purchased soon after our marriage, all six of us were at the last frontier on the Taku River across from the Taku Glacier at the Taku Glacier Lodge.

It was an almost make-believe vacation…seals in the river, moose along the banks, warm lakes, 20 hours of sunlight, and four hours of dusk. A central lodge where we partook of three family meals a day.

Our children, ages 5 to 13, were enthralled with the wonderland. We all succumbed to the same mesmerization I had earlier experienced.

It so happened that the governor's wife, a Mrs. Miller, was staying at the lodge at the same time, and one day she heard us discussing how great it would be if we could live in this beautiful state. She offered to look around for job possibilities in association management, having heard that I had been Executive Director of the Louisiana Architects' Association. Mrs. Miller also invited us to visit her at the mansion when we returned to Juneau. She left early and when we flew back to the capitol – which had a population of some 12,500 at the time – we took her up on her invitation.

While she was leading us around the mansion, she told me that the Executive Director of the Chamber of Commerce of Juneau was resigning, and she had set up an appointment for me with the president, a local physician.

After an interview and a party at his home, we returned to Baton Rouge and the real world. A week later, the call came. I had the job. Whoa!

I owned a business and had a partner. Our four parents were all living. The cost and time of flying to and from Alaska would limit our visits to funerals, plus the cost of a move by land to Vancouver and then by barge to Juneau was strictly prohibitive. I declined with pain.

In Alaska, almost all parents <u>and</u> children worked to keep pace with hyper-inflation.

In 1977, after nine years of dreaming about unattainable Alaska, a compromise presented itself. One of my clients at the time was the State Association of Louisiana Savings and Loans, whose Executive Director was Ron Albritton, a close friend and confidante.

One of our favorite pastimes was to have lunch, quickly discuss the coming issues of the organization's magazine and newsletter (which I edited), and then sit back with a glass of Mouton Cadet and dream about the day we would move out west and each buy a spread.

Sometimes our wives joined us; frazzled by the fast pace of city life, they feigned encouragement, thinking all the while that we were not serious.

At Thanksgiving of that year, Ron and his wife, Glenda, and their two children headed out to Wyoming, where it was so cold, if you spat in the snow, a marble of saliva would form on its way down to the surface. So the quartet headed south to much warmer Canon City, Colorado, where Ron went into Canon Land Company to inquire about available ranches. The receptionist explained that their "land man," John Gauss, had already left for the day, but she would be glad to have him mail some information. Ron handed her his card and headed out the front door but, before he reached the car, the lady came out yelling that John apparently had forgotten something and was parking in the back lot.

That chance meeting, hanging on a matter of seconds, transformed the lives of at least a dozen Louisianans and their families. From that get-together, Ron looked at three ranches: a 900-acre parcel just outside of Canon City, which he purchased; a 360-acre piece about 25 miles west of the city, which a mutual friend bought, and a 1,200-acre spread, 47 miles west of Canon City. When Ron returned to Baton Rouge, he called and told me about what he had found. Of course, he knew that I was land crazy. Two months later we were traveling west in my motor home to see if his enthusiasm was justified.

Before we had seen 10 percent of Little Badger Ranch (named after the creek that bisects the place), I told Mr. Gauss I wanted it.

"But you haven't seen the lodge, nor the cabins, or the lake and ponds."

"I don't care, I want it."

It was approximately the same size as Cliffwood Plantation near St. Francisville, Louisiana, which I had purchased and marketed successfully. The price per acre was the same, exactly. Cliffwood had two tenant houses, and was a series of rugged ravines so rough that we kidded about the deer getting nose bleeds. Little Badger was so peaceful, so beautiful, with its conifers and glaciers of aspens cascading from the heights; I went into that same mesmerized feeling I had experienced in Alaska. Only, here, I might own a chunk of it. It was spellbinding.

We didn't know at the time, but the reason it was so affordable had to do with a three-year drought in progress. There was little snow on the ground and we drove up to the high country with little effort.

Mr. Gauss had paid the caretaker to build fires in two fireplaces in the old lodge. He had great soup and sandwiches waiting for us.

The Hyacinth Avenue house in Baton Rouge which we sold upon going to Waveland, Mississippi, in 1974 and repurchased on return to Baton Rouge.

Massive oaks graced our home on the beach in Waveland.
Small branches had been stripped off by Hurricane Camille.

Myron Tassin, 2003

Little Badger Ranch house photographed from trout-infested lake.

Ranch house exterior / interior

Cozy living room

Built in 1929 by the homesteader, the lodge, of log construction with red cedar floors and built-ins, was very attractive to someone who wanted to leave the city. In box canyons, little valleys, on mountainsides, one could see small herds of deer grazing.

I wanted it! I wanted it! I wanted it!

In April of 1978, the act of sale went through. In June, we went with our two youngest children for the summer; Jay was 17, Ann was 15. There was no phone. There was no electricity.

We worked like sheep dogs: fixing fences, repairing eroded roads with shovels, cleaning cabins, harnessing springs for domestic water, cooking on a wood stove, earning a Ph.D. in propane refrigerator repairs, cutting some 10 cords of wood, learning to wash with an ancient generator-operated wringer washer.

The weather was so dry, a load of clothes was dry before the next load was ready for the line. We stocked the lake and ponds with rainbows, brooks and browns. They were always fresh even though our fridge might be on the fritz.

We experienced virga – rain that falls overhead but dries before reaching the ground. It was a new life – hard, but rewarding. A real adventure for a cottonpicker.

In September, we invited two couples from Louisiana, the Jim Pierson's and the August Perez's, to come visit. Perez accepted, but added emphatically, "Tassin, I'm coming, but I'm not interested in buying land." Before he left he was begging for us to form a three-way partnership on one cabin and 360 surrounding acres.

"Reluctantly," I conceded. Proceeds from that sale would pay off the rest of the ranch.

We returned at Christmastime that year, but even with a snowtrack machine we couldn't get through the four feet of white stuff at the front gate. Disappointing, but the drought was over.

In the spring of 1979, we told Anne, who was going into her junior year at St. Joseph's Academy in Baton Rouge, that if she agreed we would move in May. She took six weeks to decide, but did so in the affirmative, especially when John Gauss threw in an Arabian filly for her as an incentive.

Enrolling in St. Mary's coed academy in Colorado Springs, she fell right in with her new situation and today sees the move as one of her best decisions ever.

On weekends and holidays we went to the ranch where we just couldn't get enough of the peace and enjoyment. In May of 1979 when we went to Little Badger it was wrapped in a blanket of wet snow, under which was a growth of lush green, where it had been pretty arid the previous summer. The drought was definitely broken!

Our oldest son, Mike, who had just graduated from nursing school, came with his family to work on the ranch and study for his licensing exam.

Our second son, Tim, and his wife and son came to do construction work on our various cabins. So for a full summer, our whole family was together in this overwhelming place. Each household was in charge of supper every third evening, which provided generous recreation and leisure opportunities on your nights off.

Mike and family went back to Shreveport in the fall; Tim and Debbie and Ryan stayed on at the ranch until the snows drove them out from their wood-cutting enterprise around Thanksgiving but, before they left, we had a wonderful holiday celebration with them.

Shirley, Anne and I came from our home in Colorado Springs to spend the long week-end with them, bringing a turkey and all of the trimmings. On Thanksgiving morning, we lit the old wood stove, put the bird in the white-hot oven, filled the wood box with ponderosa pine and went out for a couple of hours of snowshoeing, sledding and ice fishing on the frozen lake, where we could catch rainbows, brooks and brown trout with corn, aluminum foil…even Big Red gum.

When we came back to the toasty Pearl Cabin, the turkey was moist, tasty and falling off the bone. If you don't believe me, ask Shirley. She can dwell on the subject for hours, especially on Thanksgiving Day when we talk about our favorite turkey of all time.

The wildlife on enchanted Little Badger Ranch included deer by the herd, elk during migration season, black bear in quantity requiring you to watch your rear as you trekked through the forest, lynx, golden and a few bald eagles, bobcat, mountain lion, badger, ferret, weasel, skunks, tree squirrels, Idaho Ground Squirrels, pack rats and mice galore, even white and black ones. (Ask Shirley.) Being at 8,500-plus feet above sea level, there were no poisonous snakes, no roaches, nor termites or poison ivy.

I saw a pair of golden eagles teaching their youngsters how to fly, a lynx perched above me on a wall of huge boulders, deer grazing placidly in the valleys, a doe dropping her fawn in our headlights, a mother bobcat trying to attract us away from her meowing kittens, a bear inches away (through a cabin window, thank goodness) and so on. It was a long way from Pollard Estates in Baton Rouge, but close to Taku River, Alaska.

As friends and business associates came to visit us, they fell in love with the peace and tranquility of this magical place and became interested in owning a little piece of this heaven. Five doctors, one architect, a savings and loan president and an attorney became members of a Louisiana community in the rocky mountains. Eventually, we owned only about 10 acres, which we gave to Tim for a Christmas present. He has since repurchased the Pearl Cabin (named after the builders and original owners) and the 120-acre box canyon that goes with it. And his parents are looking forward to spending some time in the place where we had some of our best memories and the best Thanksgiving turkey of our lives.

When Shirley's father came to visit us in the early 80's, he was still dejected from the loss of his wife and great love in 1978. As an EXXON executive for 43 years, he had traveled east but never west.

We expected him to be a "stick in the mud," but he surprised us by being so very positive and impressed with the size of the mountains and the beauty, peace and grandeur of it all, especially with the wildlife.

On the morning after his arrival, we awoke to find five huge mule deer bucks – all bucks – looking into the windows of the cabin – an occurrence which had never happened before, nor since.

Usually, when they came in the vicinity of the cabin, they stayed guardedly away, as if shying away from our presence. On that morning, they had come to pay tribute to Pappy, and I know WHO had sent them.

He took it all in stride, assuming that this was a regular treat. He died peacefully in his sleep soon after his return to Florida.

When we first moved to Little Badger Ranch, from the high country we could see a narrow valley some 40 miles south which looked like a page from a Swiss travel brochure. To the east of the valley, which appeared to be about a dozen miles wide, was a range of mountains as high as our high country (11,000 feet), but to the west, majestic peaks seemed to dwarf its sisters across the valley's green floor. From our vantage point, we could really appreciate the massive scale of the 13,000- to 14,000-foot peaks of the Sangre de Cristo Range. Little did we know we would live there for several years during the eighties and nineties.

We began attending Sunday Mass there from the Ranch, as well as from Colorado Springs when we felt like dreaming about our future. We soon decided we wanted to experience this little bit of bliss, which would put us just 40 miles from the Ranch rather than 80 as we were from the Springs.

In 1981, on the week after Anne left for her freshmen year at LSU, we moved to an old lodge which we had purchased from our friends and fellow travelers, the Ron Albrittons.

On the day we moved, a late afternoon shower left in its wake the most magnificent rainbow a mountain valley can stage, arched from the Wet Mountains on the east to the Sangres on the west.

Because of extreme elevation and little atmospheric interference, mountain rainbows are much more vivid than lowland swatches.

We held each other close on the front porch and, breathlessly, Shirley named our place "Rainbow Lodge." It was so apropos because the Rainbow Trail, a 70-mile hiking path from the southern end of the valley to the vicinity of Salida, cut through a corner of our acreage. Beyond it was the National Forest.

For the next 12 months, we fished and ice skated on the ponds, hiked and snowmobiled in the forest which stretched from our 13-acre place into hundreds of thousands of acres of accessible land. It was a simple time. Of the half dozen couples we bummed around with, five played some instrument or other, so we had lots of self-entertainment parties with great food, good grog and sparkling notes of reverie filling our little corner of the mountain kingdom.

Money kept coming in from consulting contracts and book royalties, so we weren't hungry. Besides, we did with very little. We paid $83,000 for the place and Shirley spent $10,000 on a remodeling-restoration project. We lived some eight miles from the town of Westcliffe, a former silver mining town. Our trips there were an adventurous 4-wheel drive escapade in heavy winter snow dumps of up to three feet on a given night. Deer, elk, bear and grouse frequented our yard among the aspen and spruce. Shirley, who doesn't lie, will attest to the fact that on a morning hike, a flock of grouse walked across my path. I picked up a rock and threw it and killed one for supper that evening.

Alas, I was too young and too used to working hard to play for a living. After a year of frolicking, we sold the $93,000 property for $147,500 and moved to Colorado Springs where I signed a contract to write Olympic Decathlon hero Bob Mathias' biography.

Two years later, the book completed, we moved back to a log cabin less than a mile from Rainbow Lodge. This second abode, built by the colonel who had founded the Texas Rangers, needed a "little" renovation, too. The squatter who had been living in it had a tent over his bed to shield the snowflakes from his grizzly beard. When we called on him to tell him we had purchased the place, he told us it was hallowed ground. He called himself "White Buffalo" and said he had 18 children with several squaws around the country's tribes. Shirley and I were more than a little nervous when we drove him to town to use a phone.

My "designer" did wonders with a $10,000 budget and we lived there for about four years during which time I set up an office in town to manage and market land acquisitions. We sold this jewel of a place on Short Creek to Dr. and Mrs. Jan Hildebrand of Canon City who eventually literally buried the cabin with a bulldozer and built a mini-mansion on the site, which at 9,000 feet has an unobstructed view of the valley floor below framed by the Wet and Sangre de Cristo mountains, with Pike's Peak hovering in technicolor some 65 miles to the east at Colorado Springs.

Toward the end of our tenure at Rainbow II, (a rainbow also appeared on the day we moved there), a rough, tough, jack-of-all-trades in the building industry approached me with an interesting proposition. He had found 400, 8 x 12 inch, 20-foot-long heart of Douglas fir beams in a pipe yard at La Hunta, Colorado. He would deliver them to me for $35 a beam. In them, I could already see our next Lodge.

Just up the mountain, we built Rainbow III. There was no colorful display when we moved in but a couple of days later there was one very close and unbelievably powerful. It was anchored at one end over a herd of cattle in a pasture below us, and the cows were bathed in pastel colors (ask Shirley).

Rainbow III was a 4,000-square-foot beam structure, an edifice which in reality was a lodge of straight rectangular logs. Son Tim designed it, and it was truly special with its 20 x 40 living-dining room and 20-foot cathedral ceilings as the focal point. Folks from town would drive up, make a couple of trips around the drive which circled the house and gawk through the windows, some of which were as large as 8 x 10 feet, facilitating expansive views of God's mountain wonders.

On many days, we were above the clouds. Once, I thought I could see Longbridge, Louisiana, but maybe it was the Junction. (Don't ask Shirley.)

Anne's wedding reception was held in that large room, and the ladies' high heels distressed the wide pine plank flooring with memories for a lifetime.

Friends from Baton Rouge, E. J. and Lana Cop and family, were visiting us from their cabin up the mountain one weekend. It was a very cool August day and the large stone fireplace was blazing away with the sounds of comfort. Baton Rouge was in the high 90's. E. J. and his three grown children were reclined on the carpet in front of the crackling flame and dozing off and on.

Three weeks later, Rainbow III was his, so we didn't get to enjoy the distressed floors for a lifetime. We moved up higher into his small but beautifully finished and appointed cabin which was part of the transaction. Years earlier, I had sold the parcel (on which the cabin stood along the forest beside a whispering creek) to him. Here our views were micro rather than macro.

Winters were so severe and so deep that we lengthened our annual treks to Florida. While visiting our fellow travelers, the Albrittons, who had moved back south to Shalimar, we admired the tip of the peninsula adjoining their property.

It was for sale; we bought it, eventually built a three-story seaside cottage on it, and I'm sitting at this moment writing from the third floor sunroom, glancing from time to time at the skyline of Destin across the bay. It's a crisp, cold day, but soon the warmth will spread its cozy blanket upon us, speckled trout, reds and flounder will be starving, and there will be no time for writing. In the spring, I make it a point to fish only on days that end in "Y."

For a long time we would spend nine months of each year in Colorado and three in Florida. That mix has been reversed. Three of our brood live within a day's drive (one within five minutes) and the call of loving grandchildren is a strong one, I garontee!

We've changed our sphere of operations in Colorado from the Westcliffe-Colorado Springs orbit. Our mountain home is now in Crested Butte where we were attracted by John Stroop and Carol, his wife. John and I met on his first day at LSU in 1952. We've been like brothers since. They had purchased a lot next to our beam house to retire from Atlanta someday, but they fell in love with Crested Butte, and we have, too.

We live just 2 miles from town, which is an historic district. Our church parish is small and personal and reassuring. The salmon fishing is unbelievable. In September, I caught my limit of 10 every day. You can't find better and more varied hiking trails. There's a 30-acre trout lake behind our place. The views are paralyzing. And the people are the best. Our place is modest, but fills our every need.

Two years ago, the Tassins and Stroops hiked up to the peak of Mount Crested Butte which is over 12,000 feet high, and wondered, "What are the other AARP members doing?" We plan to be buried here with our friends in the cemetery at the foot of this towering natural monument erected for the ages by you-know-WHO.

A gathering of friends on September 24, 2002 at the Crested Butte
Cemetery for a "Plot Party." Myron and Shirley Tassin, Carol and
John Stroop, Jay and Pam Jaynes, Bob and Paulette Brotherton,
Joanne and Vince Rogalski and Bev and Joe Fitzpatrick. Father Jim
Koenigsfeld was on a Sabbatical in Jerusalem and so is not pictured.
The plots are in this section of the cemetery. Each shared a short
testimony with the group about – "What if I am the first?"

Rainbow from Rainbow II

105

Rainbow II and barn are dots at base of mountain

ASPEN ALLÉE

A Rustic Mountain Lodge

Harmonious Marriage
Between Man And
Nature

Rainbow III built with over 200 8x12-inch, 20-foot-long, heart of
Douglas fir beams.

Right:
Massive,
efficient
fireplace.
Below:
Chapel vault
over
living/dining.

Rainbow III built with over 200 8x12-inch, 20-foot-long, heart of
Douglas fir beams.

Upper: Dining with the mountains as guests.
Lower: Beamed ceiling over kitchen, den.

Rainbow III built with over 200 8x12-inch, 20-foot-long, heart of Douglas fir beams.

Early summer.

Late winter.

Seasons at Rainbow III in the Sangre de Cristo Mountains.

Links Court town home on far end overlooking historic Crested Butte.

Home Sweet Home in this 500-square foot cabin for over two years.

"Fiddling on the Roof." Carpenters celebrate completion of framing phase of cottage. Magenta sky and water celebrate, too.

Steamboat Victorian cottage on Porpoise Point, Shalimar, FL.

Lights: One near. One far, rising over Destin. From our porch.

Blazing Christmas boats from Fort Walton Beach Yacht Club – with mast lights in background drawing tigers on black sky as boats bobble in the waves.

"For Thine is the Kingdom." Our resident Louisiana Heron twinkles his toes on our dock at sunrise.

"Sail-O-Wet." The Albritton's 37-footer, Sweet Caroline (named after daughter), shot from our widow's walk.

A splendid speckled trout fishing day for yours truly and friends.
Trisha Quackenbush, down-the-street friend, is wary of wriggling
creatures.

Myron Tassin, 2003

MUSINGS

GROWING UP ON THE EDGE

Before modern travel and communications amalgamated the Central Louisiana region, two worlds met just north of our Avoyelles Parish and drifted past each other like tectonic plates without ever colliding. Pronounced differences were strikingly etched north and south of an unofficial boundary delineated by the meandering Red River, flowing at that point in a west to east direction.

Going north, the world changed from short to taller people; black-haired and dark skinned to red-blond-brown hair and fair skins. "Les cou-rouge" (rednecks) we called them because the sun baked their light skin above the shirt collar to a boiled-crawfish red while ours merely turned darker.

The world changed from flat land to rolling hills; oak and other deciduous trees to piney woods; rich, fertile loam to poor red soil; Catholics to Protestants; French language and fun-loving temperament to rigid Scotch-Irish-English; imbibers to teetotalers.

It would be terribly politically incorrect today but, back then, an old ethnic joke maintained, prejudicially of course, that the dominant crops on the south side of the river were cotton and corn while on the north side they were pine cones and welfare checks.

The explanation given to me for the cultural differences was as follows: the Creole French migrated from New Orleans to the river and went no farther, and the "Tennessee Americans" migrated down to it and stopped, too, as if by unstated agreement.

Two cultures. Separated by a few hundred feet and scant minutes by rowboat. But worlds apart.

Hard work written on the face of this "Cajun." Photo by Fonville Winans whose collection is displayed in <u>We Are Acadians</u>.

CAJUN OR CREOLE?

Throughout my early years, my father always referred to our people as Creoles not Acadians (Cajuns). "What does he know," I would say to myself. I wanted to be "Cajun" because they seemed to have more fun than we Creoles.

Daddy said Cajuns were people who lived around St. Martinville, Lafayette, Breaux Bridge, Mamou, mostly in the parishes that were named after saints. They spoke a patois very different from the language spoken by the Creoles.

"Je suis un Creole," he would say proudly. He never said he was an American. To him being an American was to speak English like "Slim" Morgan who lived next door.

To be sure, there is a big migratory difference between Cajuns and Creoles. While the forefathers of the Acadians went from France to Canada to Louisiana when they were thrown out of Acadia (Nova Scotia) by the British, many French came directly from France to Louisiana and their progeny became Creole.

Although there are several definitions of the word Creole, the preceding one applies to the French people of my home parish of Avoyelles.

Our ancestors didn't stay in New Orleans, primarily because they were living in a swamp and dying like flies from mosquito-borne diseases; they moved north to Mississippi River parishes and continued to die. No one then knew that malaria and yellow fever were transported by mosquitos. The farther north they migrated, the higher the survival rate until they reached the higher prairies of Avoyelles. There they settled and stayed.

Around 1958 I met Mr. Bill Dodd, a former Lieutenant Governor, Auditor and eventually Chairman of the State Board of Education. I got to know him well when he retained me to write and produce a campaign film for him.

When he asked me where I was from, I told him I was a Cajun from Avoyelles Parish. "Were you born there?" he asked.

"Yes, I was, and my father and grandfather, too."

"You're not Cajun then. Almost all of the French people in Avoyelles are Creole, as opposed to people in the contiguous parishes of St. Landry and Evangeline."

Mr. Know-It-All was embarrassed for doubting his poorly educated but wise and intelligent father.

Webster Dictionary's definition of Creole, which applies to our people, is as follows: "A white person descended from early French or Spanish settlers of the U.S. Gulf States and preserving their speech and culture." That was Pliny and Emma Tassin to the bone.

Acadian on the other hand is defined by Webster as a Louisianian descended from French-speaking immigrants from Canada.

"A person of mixed French or Spanish and Negro descent, speaking a dialect of French or Spanish," is another definition of "Creole" given by Mr. Webster, as is also "the French dialect spoken by many Negroes in southern Louisiana."

When we moved to Colorado in the late 70's and we told a retired publishing executive living near our ranch that we were French, he asked if we were Cajuns. I told him, "No, we are Creoles." I'm sure my naturally dark skin made him scratch his head a little. Later, when he asked me to elaborate, I whipped out a copy of my book, <u>We are Acadians</u>.

The book I mention finally made me accept my father's version of the kind of French people we are. In the mid-70's, I received a contract to do a small book about the Cajuns of Louisiana. I titled the book, "<u>Nous Sommes Acadians</u>, <u>We Are Acadians</u>."

Lo and behold, in doing research for the project, I found that my ancestor, Joseph Tassin, came to New Orleans in 1722, just a couple of years after New Orleans was founded. Moves north to St. Charles and Point Coupee Parishes were apparently not satisfactory for the Tassins because these locales were, like New Orleans, inundated with regularity. Only parts of Avoyelles flooded; the prairie from Mansura north is probably 30 to 40 feet higher than alluvial lowlands. The mosquito-borne diseases diminished.

It was during the "flood of the century" in 1927 that the long wooden bridge (after which our hamlet, Longbridge, was named) was wiped out. My father watched it go.

Trees and debris came down the surging waters to form long drifts along the upstream pilings. Finally, the pressure was too intense. A new access road was built on the crest of a dike from Bayou des Glaises to the high ground of Mansura environs.

For Pliny Tassin, the loss of this important lifeline at the time would remain etched in his mind for the rest of his life.

Nous Sommes Acadiens
WE ARE ACADIANS
MYRON TASSIN

Photography by Fonville Winans

Jacket for <u>We Are Acadians</u> book, also a Fonville photo.

When it was confirmed to me that my father was right about our Creole heritage, I had to own up to the publisher, explaining to him that when I had begun the work, I had truthfully thought I was an Acadian. Now I had hard proof I wasn't. He responded quite emphatically, "For this book, Myron, you ARE an Acadian." Okay, okay, okay.

I explained that in most ways, there is little difference between Acadians and Creoles. In food, fun, temperament, joi de vivre, religion, emphasis on family – we are all French. My explanation must have been satisfactory because the book still sells today, some 24 years later.

Myron Tassin, 2003

ON BEING FRENCH

(WRITTEN IN 1997 BEFORE THE JACQUES CHIRAC-IRAQ-DEBACLE)

I've often wondered how it feels to be an Irish-American, driving along the shores of the Dingle Peninsula in the Emerald Isles...or how it feels to be a German-American sightseeing in the villages of the Bavarian Alps where famous fairy tales are illustrated by painters on the façades of local houses. How does it feel to be an Italian-American walking along the Grand Canal in Venice or an English-American witnessing the changing of the guard at Buckingham Palace? As a French-American, I felt good in these interesting places, but I didn't feel "at home."

As a French-American, surrounded by an enthusiastic crowd gathered tightly around me in a small brasserie in the town centre of Tassin, France...gathered around me because the restaurant manager had exclaimed loudly when he saw the name TASSIN on my MasterCard, I can tell you that it felt fantastic. Whether in Lyons, Paris, Dijon, or Chaumont, it felt terrific to be of French extraction. It felt like home. It's an uplifting state of mind, stimulated in me at an early age by my father, a very proud Frenchman, so you can imagine my joy in being French where it all began for us.

After having been warned for decades that the European French are haughty, unhelpful, self-centered, nose-in-the-air types, I did not expect much in the way of hospitality. WRONG!! I can't understand their politics, but I love their laissez-faire lifestyle.

More than The Louvre, Mass at Notre Dame, the Arc de Triomphe, the Eiffel Tower, countless architectural treasures,

130

vineyards to the horizon, and food and atmosphere that massage the palate and stroke the soul – more than all of these, it was the people...their friendliness, cheerfulness and helpfulness that stood out.

EXAMPLES: The taxi driver, Monsieur Baron, from the train station to our hotel in Paris, who gave us a running commentary on the sights encountered.

Monsieur Guillot, manager of the Invalides Hotel, and his staff, particularly Monsieur Didier, who went beyond the call of duty to see to our needs and wants. The hotel is not for invalids, although I wondered after dinner each evening; it was named after the gold-domed rest home which Napoleon built for his damaged minions.

Monsieur Dupont, a military writer we met in a wine bar, who went out of his way to let us know of his fondness for Americans and particularly, French-Americans.

There are Guillots, Didiers and DuPonts aplenty in my home parish in Louisiana. Naturally, I told them so, and they loved it.

Phillippe, who made us feel at home in his cozy restaurant near Notre Dame and remembered us with personal service on a subsequent visit.

I cannot forget the ordinary strangers who took great care in giving directions – even watching carefully to see that we got off the Metro at the right stop.

Nor the two old men, worshiping a couple of bottles of wine. That's right: two men, two bottles, and lunch at the neighboring table at the Poste Hotel in Saint Seine l'Abbaye. When they learned we were Americans, they joined in our conversation. One of them had earlier recommended this delightful epicurean experience and was proud as punch that we agreed with him.

Monsieur Pierrat, manager of the Louvree Hotel in Beaune, who went out of his way on a busy morning to provide comforting assistance for one in our party with a worsening cough.

The three businessmen at the next table in Sens who insisted on pouring my glass full from their unspent bottle of local wine. When I protested mildly, one of them said, "Marry me or hang me." I believe he meant that it would have hurt had we refused.

The tourist official who commented on my pack of Big Red gum, referring starry-eyed to la Dentine and memories of the GIs of WWII. Gave her my last three sticks.

The young couple named Ounis who rescued us when we missed our exit to Tassin and ended up in a park some 20 miles away. It was May 1, their Labor Day. They were killing time waiting for their young daughter to complete her nap before commencing a "piqnique" lunch.

When I approached them for directions they began exploring the possibilities. It was so complicated, they finally led us for 18 miles, hither and yon through tunnels and turnabouts, finally depositing us in the town centre of Tassin.

When they stopped, we jumped out of our car to invite them to lunch, but they already had the picnic basket in the car. Explaining that her sister had recently been to America and that she had been treated wonderfully, the young wife proceeded to invite us to dinner

Onward to Tassin, France

at their home the following night. Although we declined later by phone (we had to move on), their generosity was international relations of the best kind.

After lunch at a brasserie in the Tassin town centre, when I gave my charge card to Monsieur Frederic Gandreau, he did a double-take and exclaimed when he read the name thereon.

He wanted to know where I came from, and how it was that I spoke French. I explained that although my great, great, great, great, great grandfather, Joseph Tassin, arrived in New Orleans directly from France in the early seventeen hundreds, many of his descendants in my home parish still speak French as their first language.

Another couple – the LeFebvres – Hotel Lutetia – near Tassin. When I explained to Mme. LeFebvre that I hoped to go back to the brasserie to get the bottle of Tassin champagne promised by the manager, she insisted on handling the matter and promptly began a telephone dialogue with Monsieur Gandreau.

I can think only of one exception to the positive examples above: the creperie owner in Chaumont who persistently pressed us to order as soon as we sat down. We wanted to enjoy a bottle of wine first. We paid for the wine and departed. Of course, there are pushy people everywhere, but I wish she hadn't messed up our clean record. (The group of people who broke the line at the Eiffel Tower were Italians, so they didn't count.)

Consequently, the highlight of the trip for me, as you can tell, was the people. Those of you who are acquainted with the two ladies in our party know they are tres gentil and easy to please; just consider the men they picked.

The two husbands are completely counterbalancing: one believes everything will go wrong; the other believes everything will turn out right.

Thinking of things gone wrong, I must tell you about the andouilletes I ordered in Chaumont. I assumed they would be coarse, smoked, pork and/or beef sausage akin to our Louisiana andouilles. The "lletes" made a lot of difference. It was a pig stomach rolled up into a sausage and still reeking of its processed contents; I had but one bite of this creation, but it grew to the size of a softball before I stubbornly swallowed it and chased it down with a glass of wine. My reaction was worth the laugh...for the laughers. It happened on the same evening that we had left the demanding creperie owner. Perhaps we should have put up with her gestapo methods.

We spent too much on our first evening meal in Paris. Caught up in the romance of the moment, not to mention the fact that we were not yet at ease with the value of the French franc, we pressed merrily on. The bill exceeded the total of our hotel bill for three nights (breakfast included) in Paris. Shirley gambled with the expensive wine and won, food allergies notwithstanding. It was fit for kings, although only kings could have afforded it.

DEFINITIONS: Requesting a room with a shower at the Lutetia Hotel, the young woman came back with, "You want a douche?" I didn't think I did. It took more than a few minutes for her to convince me that in French, the word "douche" is shower. My limited vocabulary and modesty precluded explaining my confusion.

FOOD AND BEVERAGE: Pastries, everywhere, were excellent – so light they almost floated off your plate. Shirley ravaged them without adverse reaction.

Café au lait was better than New Orleans' Café du Monde. Seared and smothered rabbit was my favorite entreé. The fish from our dock is fresher, naturally. Beef and pork were average. Had duck once and it was rare, although good, but Shirley does it better. Stuffed chicken was good, but not as good as Hebert's.

We couldn't tell, and forgot to ask, if it was escargot or oysters, but the complimentary hors d'oeuvres at the Post Hotel (in a light wine, mustard, cream??? sauce) were to live for.

Overall, I must admit that Louisiana's French cuisine is mighty fair competition.

The wine was divine. No added sulfites. So now we know that Shirley's allergies from wine have nothing to do with mold.

MORE OBSERVATIONS: There was more open land than I expected. Lots of babies. Much air pollution in the cities. Lots of smokers. My Louisiana/LSU French was more than adequate. It's a more polite society. Every small town has a large church or cathedral. Dijon seemed to be exceedingly upscale. Grocery stores are very small. Although people drive very fast in cities and the countryside (we drove 80 mph in self defense on some motorways), we didn't see a single wreck in Germany or France.

IN CONCLUSION: The positive experience of getting to know a few French people overwhelmingly and thoroughly negated the false image so often perpetrated by a lemming-like U.S. media, as well as by some spoiled American tourists.

The French people, the ones we met, were wonderful to us. C'était formidable.

Even the long-ago relatives that we didn't get to meet made us feel good as well. Going to L'Arc de Triomphe and seeing Shirley's mother's maiden name, LeJeune, chiseled in stone in large letters (he was a famous French general) was a touching experience. The two LeJeune tombstones a few feet away from DeGaulle's tomb, in Colombey-les Deux Eglises, gave my heart a thump. The numerous Tassins and Ducotes and the five business places in Tassin by the same name – all of these were stirring experiences.

It was moving and touching for one who is so proud of being French.

MY GREAT HUNTING ADVENTURE WITH DADDY

So hard did my father have to work that there was little opportunity to do much in the way of father/son fun in the contemporary vernacular.

He taught me how to swim – as he sat on the bayou bank; we fished together less than a half dozen times in 18 years at home, and I can't remember hunting together until that year between high school and college.

That fateful fall week-end, I was home to wash my duds and to eat a few balanced meals when he suggested I might like to go into the denuded cotton patch and try to kill a rabbit. "Why don't we go together?" I rejoined.

We left with the double-barreled shotgun and a 22-rifle, and I have always felt that the results of our quest plainly confirmed that a Greater Power was with us on that day. Mind you, I was not much of a marksman until, as a college sophomore, I finally bought some much-needed eye glasses from a Third Street optometrist. I subsequently earned a sharpshooter's rating in the National Guard.

On that day, however, it was as if I had but to point in the direction of the quarry and I would hit my mark.

To begin with, I had the shotgun. We had barely entered the cotton rows when a rabbit with a sassy white butt took off like a streak to the right. Bam! One dead rabbit. Three doves flew overhead in overdrive. Bam, bam!! One flew on.

When we reached the meadow in the pasture, a couple of snipe or woodcocks took off from the marshy end of the crawfish pond, flying in serrated fashion just below Mach I. Bam! One stayed; the others were already zigzagging in a neighboring parish. Rabbit, dove and snipe would make an entirely edible étouffée for a starving prodigal son.

The real miracle was yet to come. Having done far better than I ever thought possible, I suggested that Daddy take the shotgun since he had not yet had a shot.

Along the edge of the cypress trees, a dove coasted in slowly to land in the top branches, spreading its wings as air breaks.

Before Daddy saw it, I took aim with the 22 and – blap – the bird miraculously fell to the ground. Hunters will know this is impossible. Daddy's eyes were the size of boiled eggs. We picked up the dove and headed on towards a flock of red-winged blackbirds, swarming in a neighbor's corn field. Bam, bam, he shot at the black cloud, and about 20 of those gumbo morsels fell to the earth; several with broken wings had to be chased down with cornstalks to put them out of their misery.

I've often wondered if God might have been telling him that, although I was a poor excuse for a farmer's son, I had a few redeeming traits, or that perhaps he had missed out on some good hunting with an "expert" as his partner.

NOTE: The reader has permission to depreciate the circumstances and discount the numbers of that day; after all, my memory of that great adventure is 51 years old, and it gets better every time I think about it.

MILITARY READINESS

In the spring of '49, I joined a Louisiana National Guard infantry unit equipped with 4.2 heavy mortars. Although the required age was 17, I joined at 16. They were hard-up for recruits; I was harder-up for spending money. My rifle was taller than I was. Attention grandchildren: Don't try such a foolish and dishonest thing.

First inspection: The captain asks, "Son, how old are you?"

"Sixteen, sir," answering loudly with authority to impress him.

"Oooh no, you're not. From now on, you're 17."

"Yes, sir," wondering if I might soon be leaving for Ft. Leavenworth.

By August, I was encamped at Fort Polk with a contingent of hardened World War II veterans as our leaders – all old enough to be my father. They were real good at "growing me up."

When I moved to Baton Rouge, I transferred to an artillery battalion and eventually worked hard enough to become a Master Sergeant. I was invited to go to officer's school, but gracefully declined. My job was assistant to the Public Information Officer, a ginger snap of a position, where I wrote articles and took photos for publication in the local papers.

Three episodes stand out in my interesting career, during which – it is important to note – our nation was never invaded:

1. On maneuvers at Fort Polk, word came down one midnight that three soldiers had jumped into a garbage pit to evade the "enemy," a pit occupied by a nest of coral

snakes. One boy died. I slept atop the cab of a large truck for three nights.

2. At a mortar demonstration by a crack regular-army unit, the powder rings for a round caught fire from excess oil in the barrel instead of igniting to propel the ammo. The shell came out of the barrel, wobbling like a wounded pintail, threatening to fall and explode within the casualty radius.

"Hit the deck," our commanding officer yelled. Two of us plunged under a medic's jeep. With fingers jammed into my ears up to the second joint, I couldn't hear a thing. I looked toward my fellow "plunger" and saw that he was bleeding profusely in the face. "Oh, my God," I thought, "I might be wounded and dying too, but I'm so scared, I must not have heard the explosion because I've lost my sense of hearing."

It seems my buddy had run into the handles of one of the stretchers on the back of the jeep and had torn a gash into one of his temples. The shell had indeed fallen within the casualty range, but it had not rotated forcefully enough to sling out the firing pin to arm it.

3. From Fort Bliss, Texas, we used an artillery range in Alamorgordo, New Mexico. By then, I was Assistant Public Information Officer and, like a peacetime Ernie Pyle (more like Gomer Pyle), I walked around with a 4 x 5 Speed Graphic camera awaiting my big break.

Our cannon were firing at drone planes, which I confess they seldom hit. Shrapnel from a near miss must have finally hit something in the engine of one of the drones, and it began flying in erratic fashion like a wounded snipe toward White Sands Proving Grounds, which we could see from the range tower some 60 miles away.

We neither saw nor heard the wounded drone for a half hour or so and thought it had run out of fuel. We were wrong; someone in the tower began frantically yelling and pointing to a dot in the sky. It was headed right for our firing lines, probably owing to a homing device. It crashed under the rear of a nearby 2½-ton troop carrier with a full load of men waiting to evacuate but didn't even break a single fingernail, leaving the troops with pancake makeup from the cloud of fine sand mixed with panicking perspiration.

"This is my big scoop," I thought, from my distance of about 100 yards. Running up to the smoldering, mangled drone, I began taking a bunch of pictures. Our commanding officer came racing up to me, puffing out a barrage of words. "Tassin, what are you doing?"

"Taking photos for my releases, sir."

"Give me that camera and those film holders. This never happened."

Methodically, he pulled the sheets of negative film from the holders, held them up to the singeing, searing, bright, high-desert light, saying, "This one doesn't have a picture on it. Neither this one. Oops, this one doesn't either"…until they were all exposed to the blinding light…except for one that he overlooked and, although I processed it in the lab, I could never use it. Didn't want to lose my stripes. He didn't want to do the dreaded paper work with nine carbon copies.

NATIONAL GUARD BUREAU

REPORT OF SEPARATION AND RECORD OF SERVICE IN THE ARMY NATIONAL GUARD OF THE UNITED STATES AND THE ARMY NATIONAL GUARD OF LOUISIANA

AND AS A RESERVE

TYPE OF DISCHARGE HONORABLE

(No erasures or alterations in this entry enltd)

1. NAME *(Last, first, middle initial)*	2. SERVICE NO.	3. GRADE	4. ARM OR SERVICE	5. TERM OF ENLISTMENT
TASSIN, Myron J	25 504 833	M/Sgt	Artillery	Three (3) Yrs

6. ORGANIZATION Hq Btry 769th AAA Bn (AW)(M)	7. DATE OF DISCHARGE	8. PLACE OF DISCHARGE
HOME STATION Baton Rouge, La.	3 July 1958	Baton Rouge, Louisiana

9. PERMANENT ADDRESS FOR MAILING PURPOSES	10. DATE OF BIRTH	11. PLACE OF BIRTH
935 Violet St., Baton Rouge, La.	6 Feb 1933	Cottonport, Louisiana

12. CIVILIAN OCCUPATION *(Include name and address of present employer, or if unemployed, the last employer)*
Public Relations - United Givers fund - Baton Rouge, La.

13. RACE			14. MARITAL STATUS			15. U. S. CITIZEN	
WHITE	NEGRO	OTHER *(Specify)*	SINGLE	MARRIED	OTHER *(Specify)*	YES	NO
X				X		X	

16. COLOR EYES	17. COLOR HAIR	18. HEIGHT	19. WEIGHT	20. NO. DEPENDENTS
Hazel	Black	5 FT. 6½ IN.	156 LBS.	Three (3)

MILITARY HISTORY

21. DATE AND PLACE OF ENLISTMENT	22. MILITARY OCCUPATIONAL SPECIALTY AND NUMBER
4 July 55 - Baton Rouge, Louisiana	Operations Sergeant - 163.60

23. MILITARY QUALIFICATION AND DATE *(i. e., Infantry, Aviation, Marksmanship Badges, etc.)*
Sharpshooter - US Carbine cal 30 - 12 Jul 57

24. DECORATIONS, CITATIONS, MEDALS, BADGES, COMMENDATIONS, AND CAMPAIGN RIBBONS AWARDED OR AUTHORIZED *(This period of service)*
Sharpshooter Medal - US Carbine cal 30

25. PRIOR SERVICE *(Branch of service, inclusive dates, and primary duty with MOS)*
Army (NGUS) - 4 Jul 49 to 3 Jul 52 - Unk
Army (NGUS) - 4 Jul 52 to 3 Jul 55 - Unk

26. RETIREMENT CREDITS EARNED *(This period of service)*

FIRST YEAR			SECOND YEAR			THIRD YEAR			TOTAL POINTS THIS SERVICE
FROM—	TO—	POINTS	FROM—	TO—	POINTS	FROM—	TO—	POINTS	
4Jul55	3Jul56	75	4Jul56	3Jul57	76	4Jul57	3Jul58	76	227

27. LENGTH THIS SERVICE			28. TOTAL SERVICE FOR PAY PURPOSES			29. LATEST IMMUNIZATION DATES				30. HIGHEST GRADE HELD
YEARS	MONTHS	DAYS	YEARS	MONTHS	DAYS	SMALLPOX	TYPHOID	TETANUS	OTHER *(Specify)*	
3	0	0	9	0	0	May56	May56	Jun56	None	M/Sgt E7

31. SERVICE SCHOOLS ATTENDED AND DATES	32. EDUCATION *(Years)*		
	GRAMMAR	HIGH SCHOOL	COLLEGE
None	8	4	4

33. REASON AND AUTHORITY FOR DISCHARGE
Expiration Term of Service para 6 SO 112 AGO La

34. REMARKS *(This space for completion of above items or entry of other items specified in NG directives)*
EM not available for signature

35. SIGNATURE OF PERSON BEING DISCHARGED *(Full name)*	36. SIGNATURE OF OFFICER AUTHORIZED TO SIGN *(Type name, grade, and organization)*
	Don Cannon Jr
	DON CANNON JR
	Capt Hq Btry 769th AAA Bn (AW)(Mbl)

NGB FORM 22
15 NOV 49

16-60450-1 ☆ U. S. GOVERNMENT PRINTING OFFICE : 1956 O - 313135

Military Discharge Form

HUNGER PAINS

Have you ever been hungry, not knowing whence the next five meals will come?

It happened to me during that first summer in Baton Rouge. With only change left in my pocket, I decided on Friday not to go back to Longbridge for the weekend, figuring I could borrow a few bucks from some of my friends until Monday's payday. Poor planning. They had all decided to go back to the country.

On Friday night, I spent my remaining funds on an abbreviated supper. Saturday morning, the sun was shining brightly, the birds were singing energetically and my stomach was moaning loudly; by Saturday noon, the beast was growling.

On Saturday night, I was getting a little weak and drank several glasses of water before I drifted into fitful sleep. I had spent most of the day walking around on Third Street, the shopping district, hoping to spot someone I knew, even casually. Nobody.

On Sunday morning, I doubled up on the glasses of water, thinking that they would at least give me a full feeling for a few minutes. I was filling the wrong tank, but at least I wasn't dehydrating. I went back to Third Street and thought of washing dishes for a snack but kept on walking. Window shopping is not very nourishing. Every minute became like 10; my stomach acids were devouring my inner lining.

My guardian angel must have been working overtime that weekend. At about three o'clock I saw a man from the Cottonport area. I didn't know him but knew of him as a cheerful, colorful, carefree character who walked on the edge of the wild side.

He used to drive from the Hickory area through Longbridge to the bars in Mansura. On our gravel road, he drove at speeds that could have qualified him for the pole position in the Indianapolis 500.

When I approached him, my pride had long been relegated to the backseat. The search for sustenance was foremost on the agenda.

"Mr. Ducote, you don't know me, but I'm from Cottonport – actually Longbridge." (I've always been a namedropper.) "I've run out of money, my friends are all gone, and I don't get paid until Monday."

"How much do you need?"

"A dollar will do just fine." Remember, this was 1951.

I knew there was an early franchise eatery down the street named the Toddlehouse (or was it the Humpty Dumpty?) where you could get a really good burger, a slice of banana cream pie and a small drink for a buck.

He whipped out his wallet and handed me not one, but <u>two</u> dollars. I thanked him profusely, assuring him I would repay him promptly.

"Take your time," he replied. Before he headed on his way, I got his address.

Restraining myself from breaking into a mad run, I walked briskly toward the fast food joint. With that amount, I could buy two hamburgers, french fries, the pie and a "big" orange.

And I did. And it was delectable. Escargot as an appetizer, a sensation salad, followed by medium-rare chateaubriand attended by parsleyed garlic potatoes and a medley of veggies sauteed in lemon butter sauce could not have been better.

In a few short years, after relentless, dogged pursuit, Ray Ducote would marry my friend and benefactor, Catherine Hollis. And now you know the rest of Ray's story.

I would get to know him better, and to all of his sans souci traits, I would add GENEROSITY. God bless you, Ray.

(Incidentally, Ray spells his last name thusly: DuCoté. Of course, he's from the aristocratic Ducotes.)

DREAM MEALS

Having been <u>REAL</u> hungry once was enough.

Sprinkled throughout these pages is testament to the legendary importance of food to the French, and to this Frenchman. Staying true to this borderline obsession, I have enjoyed playing a game at parties where the participants are asked to declare their favorite top ten meals.

These are my ten, not necessarily in the order of preference:

Crawfish étouffée; pork neck-bone (or chicken) turnip fricassée; roast Long Island Duckling over rice with sweet garlic tomato gravy as a side sauce; steamed Blue, Alaskan King or Dungeness crab with white corn-on-the-cob; sautéed fish filets (speckled trout, redfish, red snapper, black snapper, flounder, grouper or bass); lump crabmeat in lemon-butter-green onion sauce on pasta; deep-sea, Ruby Red shrimp en brochette; grilled rack of lamb with baked brown-sugared acorn squash; garlic-stuffed pork rib roast over rice; seafood gumbo with crabmeat, shrimp, oysters.

All of the above enhanced by Shirley's green salad with sweet lemon French dressing.

BOOKS

Since 1968, I have written or co-written and published over 20 books. Subjects have ranged from architecture, Mardi Gras; Proud, Peculiar New Orleans; steamboating era, street cars, sports, Arabian horses, various places, the Grand Ole Opry and the Acadians.

This is my last one. I mean it!

"Why Me, Lord"

Myron Tassin, 2003

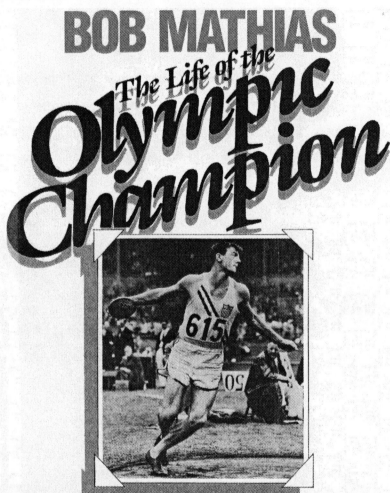

Bob Mathias book jacket

BACCHUS

By MYRON TASSIN
With an Introduction to Mardi Gras by FRANCES PARKINSON KEYES

Bacchus book jacket

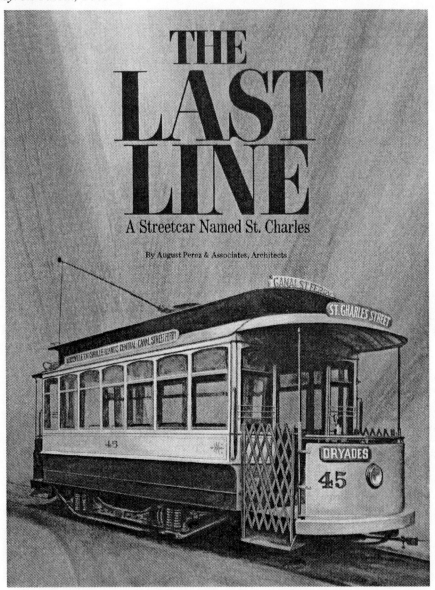

"The Last Line" book jacket

Fifty Years at the
GRAND OLE OPRY

By Myron Tassin and Jerry Henderson

Foreword by MINNIE PEARL

Introduction by MOTHER MAYBELLE CARTER

"Grand Ole Opry" jacket

WHERE WAS I WHEN ...

...The terrorist crimes of 9-11 were perpetrated?

Asleep in our place in Crested Butte. Anne, Brent and the girls were en route to visit with us. The phone jerked me out of some placid dream, probably the one with me as a forest ranger traipsing about with the wild creatures in the aspen forest behind our place.

She was calling from Ouray, Colorado, where they had spent the night. Anne: "I'm sick." I thought she had the typical travelers' virus or sore throat.

"You don't know do you?"

...President Kennedy was shot?

At noon Mass at St. Joseph's Cathedral in Baton Rouge. Shirley and I were going to have our first lunch out together since Anne's arrival. We met at church and went back to eat at the Jack Tar Hotel where my Architects' Association offices were located.

When we walked into the lobby, TV's were blaring, crowds were hanging around the sets, and the viewers' faces said, "Stunned." "Shocked."

...President Roosevelt declared war after Pearl Harbor was attacked?

In a sizeable crowd in our front yard on the Bayou at Longbridge. I was eight. Our battery-powered radio was sitting on a kitchen chair on the front porch. When those famous words about "infamy" were spoken, the men began milling around, looking down at their scuffed farmer's shoes, probably trying to assimilate and decipher the meaning of it all. The women began to cry as if somehow instantly interpolating the implications of the situation and what it portended for their husbands, sons, uncles, nephews, cousins, neighbors, nation...

... December 1941

"Day of Infamy"

PEARL HARBOR ATTACKED

War Declared

... November 1963

KENNEDY SLAIN

Johnson Sworn In

... September 2001

Terrorists Strike U.S.

THOUSANDS BELIEVED DEAD

MALAPROPS, MIXED METAPHORS AND CONVOLUTED SAYINGS

Our dear friend, Mae Martin, had a quick mind, so quick in fact that her mouth couldn't keep up with her thoughts. For years, I kept a card in my wallet to jot down some of her best lines, teasing her that I would someday publish a book on this phenomenon. "Oh, you know what I mean," she would retort with smiling, sparkling eyes.

Sad to say, Mae departed our midst to join her Maker and husband Earl before I had enough material for a book, but here are examples of her malapropisms and typical comments.

"You can't change horses on the other side of the stream."

Who sez?

"Right away, I could read the writing between the walls."

You could?

"He's so unreliable, he can't eat the mustard."

Why not?

"It goes in one ear and out one side of his mouth."

Really?

"I was still in bed that morning, sound awake."

Hmmm.

Sidney Gray, another great friend and client (when he was executive director of the Louisiana Municipal Association) used to chop, dice and mix metaphors:

"A rolling stone is worth two in the bush."

"A bird in the hand can be very messy."

"Show me a home where the buffalo roam, and I'll show you a dirty house."

My brother's brother concocted these sayings:

"Is" is still "is;" in fact, "was" used to be "is."

"If you come to a fork in the road, by all means take the 'right' one."

"Never go into the cattle business when you live in the city."*

"Don't go into the ski resort business if your feet tend to get cold."*

"Money is not important until you have a toothache."*

"If you insist on backing into your second car,* please reduce speed."

"An apple a day is too much."

"If you get a lemon, make a soufflé."

"Life is just a bowl of gumbo."

"Variety is the spice of jambalaya."

"Before you hide your lamp under a bushel basket, mail in your fire insurance premium."

*Been where? Done what?

THE NAME OF THE GAME

Once upon a time, I invented a word game. You gave a fictitious person's first name and a hint, and the other players had to decipher the person's last name, i.e. "Ron A. __ __ __ __ is out of control. His last name is M U C K.

It was to be a board game, or a newspaper cartoon quiz.

With over 1,000 name combinations, I figured some game company would be irrepressibly interested.

Wrong again!

An editorial cartoonist for the Colorado Springs Gazette became interested in the project, became my partner and illustrated it, drew up a game board, and all that jazz. IT FLOPPED, or perhaps we might say, "It has not yet been sufficiently appreciated."

A few examples are herewith included to make me feel that all the expense and effort were not totally in vain, sort of like a woodworker who builds a piece of furniture that won't sell, but he keeps it in a corner of the shop to admire.

Game sample

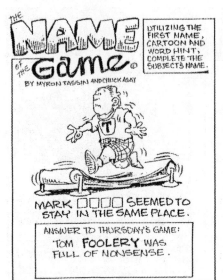

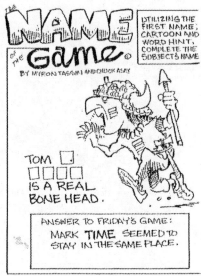

Game sample

Game sample

Game sample

Game sample

ASSAULT ON THE SENSES

To grow up on a farm is difficult, but it can be a blessing as well. Would urban children have their senses assaulted, aroused and honed from such a confluence of compelling catalytic forces? Forces and observations like...

Old life in the previous year's turned-under, decomposing corn stalks, engendering new life in tender green spring shoots. Newly-tilled earth with uncovered grubs and earthworms burrowing frantically to escape the bright light of day and the beaks of crows, grackles and mockers.

A swampy crawfish slough with decaying plant life at the shallow end and a partially submersed coon carcass against the far bank (salad AND meat for the "mudbugs.")

The difference between the unremarkable smells of vegetable blossoms and the enchanting fragrance of blooming fruit orchards.

The dichotomy of coaxing sweet, white milk from a stinking, steaming, rain-soaked, loose-boweled cow.

Pink, suckling piglets with white bubbles of froth on their frosted vests. Pungent, fresh manure and less smelly cured cakes, and the correlation between diet, its processor and odor.

Arresting jasmine after dark; early morning bitter weed...bitter even in smell.

An acre of shallots making you hungry for dirty rice dressing.

May peaches advertising their unmistakable perfume.

Dryness of pecans, walnuts, and peanuts in the fall; the wetness of plump fruit and vegetables in the summer.

Contrast between the pungent, sickening odor of wet chicken feathers being plucked, and the appetizing, mellow, "mouth-sweating" aroma of étouffée in the black skillet.

Sounds of lovelorn frogs, a hard summer's rain on a zinc roof, the bellow of a heifer at the moment of first birthing, a stallion's call to a neighbor's mare in estrus, sparrows eating cracked corn in the chicken yard, mallards on a November pond, snow geese veeing to Southwest Louisiana for a mild winter vacation, moths and hungry birds vying for nectar in Mama's flower beds.

Acorns falling softly, but audibly, onto the forest floor. Robins fighting over a holly tree, dogs quarreling over a ham bone, pigs squealing over a cow plop, pigeons cooing over their corpulent squabbling squabs. A February wind auditioning in morose F minor through the sycamore tree in the barnyard. The forlorn lowing of a calf separated from his mother at weaning time.

Buzzards coasting high and lazily in search of the next meal. A hawk swiping a spring pullet in the yard in front of your disbelieving eyes. Perch following your naked hook up to the surface, over-anxious for the next course.

Rows of waving cornstalks, teasing empty stomachs.

Swallows lining up neatly along electrical lines. Returning to their spring-summer houses, chattering, twittering purple martins celebrating a migrational tradition and an abundant mosquito crop.

A day-breaking, ear-piercing mockingbird presenting a monotonous curtain-raising revue.

Affirming that grass is always greener, Old Jim leaning hard over the top strand of barbed wire while Nancy-the-mare reverses the effort from the other side.

Creaks from Daddy's rocking chair as he piles up mileage on the living room linoleum.

Mama's peaceful countenance and moving lips while saying her third rosary of the day. (The prevailing belief insisted that to say proper prayers, the lips had to move. To "think" the prayer was not sufficient. I felt that if God could see what was in my heart and soul, he would know what was on my mind.)

Frenzied procreation in plain sight among fowl, swine, equine, bovine, dogs, cats, flocks, herds, coveys, schools, litters, gaggles (and two possums in a pecan tree); local, regional, national, world-wide, presumably all with variations on the theme of survival of the species. The pain of birth, the innocence of offspring, and the demonstrative affection of most parents.

Can one be exposed to and absorb such knowledge and experiences in a teeming city – before reaching adolescence? Why me, Lord?

THE JOY OF SINGING

There's an old gospel hymn entitled something like "I Just Can't Keep from Singing." I have that problem almost every day. While it's a joy for me, it's a curse for those around me, because much of it is subconscious.

My singing, whistling or humming gets old for my sweetheart, especially when I get stuck on the same song for hours, at which time she will patiently but firmly ask me to "Change the tune, please!"

The credit for my love of singing must be attributed to my father who could play the harmonica, the fiddle and a little guitar...all by ear. When we were down and out in the cottonpatch, singing was useful and enjoyable self entertainment. He would usually do a solo and the rendition would be followed with offerings by other individuals during which our spirits would be lifted with each note emitted, and better morale made for better pickers.

Mama didn't sing, except when rocking her babies. I don't sing very well but I like to do it, so much so that I will even wake up at night with a song on my mind.

Although I don't read music, I've been singing in choirs since early elementary. In the second grade, I sang my first solo at St. Mary's in Cottonport. It was supposed to be a duet, but my partner chickened out after a couple of lines so I kept on going. I believe the hymn was "Mother Dear, Oh Pray for Me," and Mama flooded the pew with a puddle of tears. After the attack on Pearl Harbor, I sang at a war bond rally at the movie theater in Cottonport. Dressed in a little sailor suit, I belted out "Anchors Aweigh." Yes, Mama boo-hooed again. At one time, I was singing in two choirs in the Ft. Walton Beach area and one in Crested Butte, Colorado.

Several years ago, I composed a song entitled "Christmas Melody," a fantasy about being in Bethlehem on the night Jesus was born. Later I wrote new words when Mother Teresa died, imagining her joyous reception into Paradise.

Altogether I've composed eight or nine, several of them based on bible passages – like the Feast at Cana, Zacchais climbing the sycamore tree, forgiveness, loaves and fishes, an Easter song, and my favorite: "Did You Help to Carry the Cross (the Day the Lamb Was Slain)," a Good Friday song. Some have been sung in churches in three states.

How do I compose without reading music? Fair question. We have an old pump organ and with the help of stickers, I have numbered the notes, and use that reference point until I have a creation down pat. I then record it and send the tape to a friend in Baton Rouge, who is a music teacher and computer whiz.

With a miraculous program, he feeds in the notes and chords, selects the musical instruments – horns, strings, drums, whatever he wants for accompaniment – and PRESTO, he has a computer orchestra playing my stuff. On command, the computer prints out the sheet music for the piece.

For someone who is computer illiterate, it's magic. Following are the music and words for some of my favorites. Perhaps one of you grandchildren can get one published someday. While you're at it, please get my Name Game produced and marketed.

Myron Tassin, 2003

The Day The Lamb Was Slain

by Myron Tassin
June24, 00

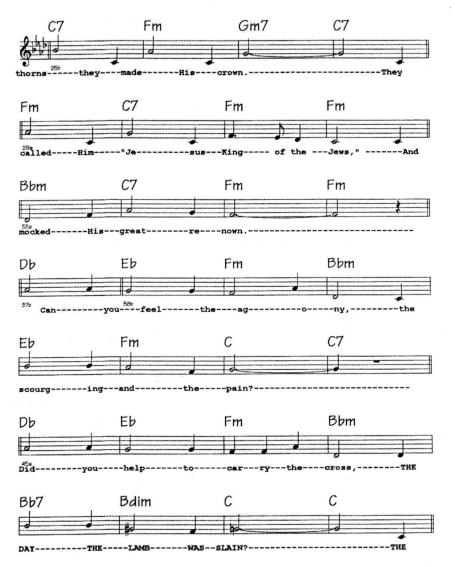

The Day The Lamb Was Slain - Page 2

The Day The Lamb Was Slain - Page 3

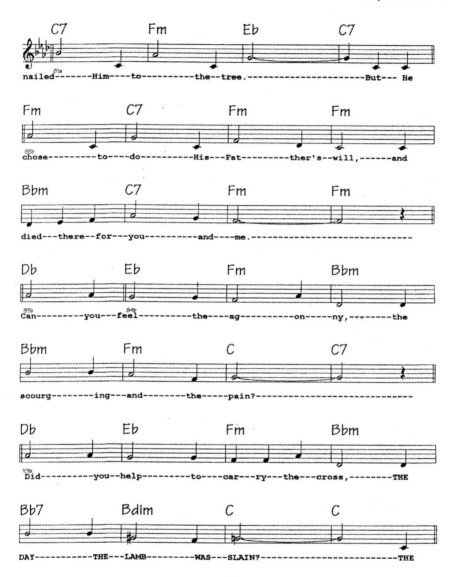

The Day The Lamb Was Slain - Page 4

Myron Tassin, 2003

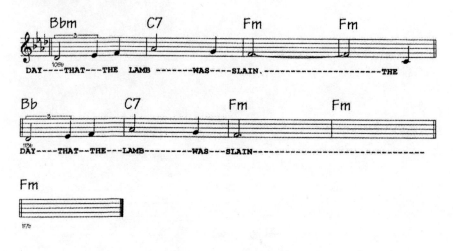

Bbm   C7   Fm   Fm

DAY----THAT---THE LAMB --------WAS----SLAIN.----------------------THE

Bb   C7   Fm   Fm

DAY----THAT--THE---LAMB---------WAS---SLAIN----------------------------

Fm

SAMARITAN

By Myron Tassin, Copyright 1997

Tell me dear Lord, who is my neighbor?
Could it be, Lord, that he's a stranger.
Is it the priest, who came by that day?
Who saw I was injured, but still went away.

Is it the Levite, who came by that place?
Surely he saw the pain on my face.
He made no attempt to offer his aid.
No gesture, no feeling, no effort was made.

Who poured the oil on my sad affliction?
Who bound my wounds with tender compassion?
He took me to shelter and paid for my care.
He could have done nothing, but did twice his share.

REFRAIN:

Who is my neighbor? It's quite plain to see:
He does works for you, Lord, as he does them for me.
He took me to shelter, and paid for my care.
He could have done nothing, but did twice his share.

Myron Tassin, 2003

Lead Us, Jesus, When We Sing (piano sheet)

Key of Ab

by Myron Tassin (c) 1997

LEAD US, JE_SUS, WHEN WE SING. Let our voic-es ring, ring, ring!
Hum-ble notes to you we bring, Like the songs of birds in spring.
High so--pranos with des-cants, Al--tos har-mo--niz-ing chants,

Like the bells on Eas-ter morn, On the day our faith was born.
Let us sing from ev'ry pew, Let us sing for You, You, You!
Bass-es deep like an-cient lutes, Let the ten---ors sing like flutes.

Christ is ris-en from the dead,   Ris-en as He sure-ly said.

Let us al   par--ti-ci-pate,   Let us sing and cel-e-brate!

cel---------e--------brate!-------------------------

Lead Us, Jesus, When We Sing (piano sheet) - Page 2

Myron Tassin, 2003

IMAGINE TERESA

1.   Imagine Teresa in paradise,
      To meet our blessed Lord.
      When she arrives, the heavens resound,
      With God's universal chord.

Refrain:

> *With notes of love and charity,*
> *Peace and purity,*
> *They sing of all her selfless work,*
> *For those in poverty. In perfect harmony.*

2.   The angels know that she has arrived;
      They hover all above.
      And Gabriel blows his heavenly horn,
      In tones of celestial love.

Refrain

3.   She sees a sea of chosen ones,
      As vast as it can be.
      The multitude of heavenly hosts,
      Cheers her in ecstasy.

Refrain

4.   Pure bliss and rapture fill them all;
      Her soul is brightest light.
      They sing with tidings of gladness and joy:
      Our sister is home tonight!

Refrain

THE FIRST MIRACLE

Jesus and Mary came to be,
At a wedding feast in Galilee.
The wine ran short, but Mary knew,
Her Son would see them through.

They have no wine she told her Son,
Whose public life had not begun.
What wouldst thou have me do woman,
My hour has not yet come;

There were six jars in front of them;
Attendants filled them to the brim.
He changed the water into wine·
A wine declared quite fine.

Refrain: From the water, he made a wine so good,
           But Jesus fully understood,
           That his long, hard trip to Calvary
           Began that day in Cana, Galilee.

FAMOUS FRIENDS

All of us know great people: a spouse, offspring, a teacher, coach, friend. Some have the good fortune to know individuals who are not only great but famous as well, and I have been blessed with that privilege.

By "knowing," I refer not to casual acquaintances. (Friends of mine and I once spent a half hour chatting casually with Bob Hope, but I don't see that as "knowing" someone.) I mean friends who enjoy receiving you into their homes and who likewise honor you with visits; people who break bread and celebrate with you, who give to you and receive graciously in return – over an extended period of time.

These stand out:

WILLIAM D. BORDERS, Priest, Monsignor, Bishop and, finally, Archbishop of Baltimore, the oldest Catholic Diocese in America. Beyond that, his credits include officiating at our wedding Mass when he was Chaplain of Christ the King Chapel at LSU.

JAMES GUIRARD, a Washington, D.C. attorney and former Chief-of-Staff to U.S. Democratic Senators Allen Ellender and Russell Long of Louisiana; founder and president of the TrueSpeak Institute, a private organization devoted to truth-in-history and truth-in-language in public discourse.

Through long hard work, determination, loyalty and abundant native intelligence, DONALD JONES, ascended from sales clerk to regional manager of several multi-state, even multi-country territories of retail giant, Sears Roebuck & Co. In his last assignment, he was responsible for outlets with 17,000 employees and sales volume of $1 1/2 billion.

FATHER JAMES MAHRER was 93 years old and still the active pastor of Assumption Catholic Church in Westcliffe, Colorado, when he died. A dear friend, he was believed to be the oldest active parish priest on the planet.

MAJOR GENERAL DONALD MARKS, United States Air Force (Ret), a command pilot with over 8,500 flying hours, including 355 hours in combat. The General rose up the chain of authority from squadron and wing command positions to Chief of Staff of the Strategic Air Command, where he directed staff operations with a 2,000 member staff and a quarter billion dollar budget.

BOB MATHIAS, twice Olympic gold medal winner of the decathlon and world record holder, considered to be the greatest all around athlete up to that time.

LIEUTENANT GENERAL HAL MOORE, of blockbuster book and movie fame ("We Were Soldiers"), considered the most successful and famous U.S. military leader of the Vietnam War.

THE TAYLOR BOYS. Brothers Gene and Dean – sons of Penny and Gary Taylor (my former boss) – moved next door to us in Baton Rouge in 1960 when Gene was eight and Dean, 13. Our two oldest sons were younger than Gene but tried to keep up with this bright, precocious child. Today, the independent-thinking Democrat is in his eighth term in Congress representing a southern Mississippi district. Dean is chief executive officer of Tidewater, Inc. (Tidewater Marine) with its worldwide operations, 8,000 employees and 24,000 dependents.

'Tis oft-said that behind each great man is a great woman. Shouldn't that be transposed? That certainly is the case with Ruth Curl Guirard, Jackie Jones, Sue Marks, Gwen Mathias, Julie Moore, and Archbishop Borders who – while he doesn't have a wife – certainly has a spouse, the Catholic Church, and he has been its stalwart partner. That went for Father James, too.

With Bob Mathias, we share our crawfish étouffée while he showers choice writing assignments, his friendship and rich anecdotes of an incomparable international and historic life...all the while reveling in down-to-earth, common-man matters like an old wood cooking stove for his mountain cabin.

Besides his wild mushrooms and my fresh-caught salmon and Louisiana gumbo, Hal Moore shares his table, friends and deep abiding faith, plus his heroic aura – which his overflowing natural humility cannot contain. His presence projects.

In addition to his love of French culture, food and friends, Jim Guirard lets us share in his important work by giving us the privilege of editing many of his brilliant works. This Fulbright scholar has an immense head, and it is chock full of brainpower.

In our years of fishing together, Don Jones and I have fed enough shrimp and bull minnows to bay aquatic population to keep Roy Ledbetter's Salty Bass Baithouse just barely off the New York Stock Exchange.

Archbishop Borders has been a leader in church councils throughout his long career, but has maintained the personal parish priest contact with the vast number of souls who have come under his care. Always modest and self-effacing, he has uncommon wisdom and invincible optimism in the goodness of man and the rewards to come.

Shirley sandwiched between Bob and Gwen on widow's walk.

Don Marks calls every few days. "Just checking in," he says. Just checking on his friends to see if they might need something. Like General Moore, his outstanding past achievements are of little consequence to him. We break bread often.

We stay in touch with the Taylor "boys" and their achievements through their dad.

Father James' rectory was an apartment adjoining the church. During Mass, you could smell the tantalizing aroma of the duck he was roasting in the oven. At Communion, he would often issue a whispered invitation to the feast. He did all of his cooking 'til the end and mowed the church lawn until he was in his high eighties.

It goes without saying that knowing famous people does not by any means make one famous, but it is so interesting and instructive to observe how many of the truly renown are self-effacing, self-satisfied, comfortable in their own skin and generous with their talents and rewards.

THE JOHN T. HILLS: A BLESSING

How fortunate can one be? You have this wonderful, loving family. You get married and then you have two wonderful, loving families. It happened to me.

Shirley's parents were as close to me as if they had been my blood parents, and her siblings treated me as one of their own. I will forever be grateful to Mr. And Mrs. Hill (Pappy and Mammy), Neff Lynn, Elaine, J. T., and Ray and their spouses, Eileen, Perry, Barbara, and Jean.

The John T. Hills.

(Shirley on mother's knee.)

THE BIG FAILURE

Everything is NOT perfect in this paradise!

For a long time, I've been trying to analyze why our generation has been such an abysmal failure in passing on to our progeny our deep commitment to the Faith of our Fathers.

I firmly believe that for 2,000 years, our religion has been a major component in the lives of our ancestors. For a hefty majority of the new generation, this bright flame of faith appears to be flickering.

Yes, the young believe yet in God but are not too keen on "the Church" and religion. What a solemn and weighty liability it is to have to face the fact that by our very omissions and/or commissions, we will be the first generation in these 20 centuries to be responsible for breaking that tradition to our bloodlines' distant past. Are we ready to defend that reality in a "higher" court?

Some blame this turn of events on popular culture, modern society, better communications, better educated people. I blame it on less committed parents; i.e., I blame it on me. And I find no solace in numbers. The fact that it is a widespread phenomenon does not obliterate the fact that I am still responsible for MY family.

You hear, "I wish our priest would give better sermons." I want to say, "You want entertainment, go to the movies." Some say, "My church is a mountain lake, or an aspen forest, or the beach at sunrise." I want to scream, "Can you receive the sacraments at the lake, forest or beach?"

Church, sermons and sacraments vis-à-vis places of refreshing solitude and contemplation are not mutually exclusive; one can do both.

By the sacraments, I mean the once-in-a-lifetime ones like Baptism, First Communion, Confirmation, Matrimony, Holy Orders (for some), but especially the oft-experienced sacraments of Holy Eucharist and Reconciliation...that fortify us with the grace to save our immortal souls.

Christ didn't say "Come and enjoy the peace and quiet of this aspen forest and do this in memory of me." With the doctrine of transubstantiation, the Eucharistic elements of bread and wine become the blood and body of our Lord. He told us to eat of it, and to do so in memory of Him. He didn't perform this miracle for the Last Supper alone. When He said, "Do this in memory of <u>Me</u>," He was saying that it should be done over and over again throughout the ages.

You wonderful grandchildren might enjoy this story my mother (who believed in a loving, but also a stern, judgmental God) told me at a tender age when I asked her how long eternity is. "If a dove, once each year, flies to a planet the size of the Earth and flaps its wings once, brushing the tips on the surface of that planet and then flies away...when the planet is totally eroded by the actions of the dove, that's the BEGINNING of eternity. That's a long time to be in any uncomfortable place."

I try to find solace in the fact that our children are all good, upstanding, hardworking, honest, loving – very loving – people, and if God is Love, as our faith teaches and we believe, and if our faith is based on loving God, our neighbor and ourselves (as He stipulated when asked about the commandments), then there is reason to be hopeful. Yet, it is presumptive and worrisome to believe I could not have done it better – much, much better.

POST SCRIPT: Although unsuccessful to a significant degree, our generation <u>DID</u> try to propagate the faith among the next. Question is: WHAT WILL THIS NEXT GENERATION DO?

EPILOGUE: LOVE AND MARRIAGE

"You sure did marry up," the chairman of the committee which selected me for the United Givers Fund job in 1955 told me many years later, and he was right.

Shirley, a native of Baton Rouge, graduate of St. Joseph's Academy, student at LSU (until love interfered), the perfect mother, a lasting friend, a patient and forgiving confidant, sweet and attractive and desirable – has been my soul mate for almost 50 years (not including two before marriage).

It's true: opposites do attract. (See chart below.)

Shirley	Myron
Introvert	Not
Even-tempered	Not
Soft-spoken	Not
Self-satisfied	Overly Ambitious
Private	Gregarious to a fault
Patient	Working on it
Gentle	Periodically
Relaxed	Let's stir the pot
Attractive (very)	Can wiggle his ears
Refined	Can whistle in French

She was 16; I was 18. And fortunate.

We had met in August of '51, that first year in Baton Rouge, when Norris Marchand, a Revenue Department summer student employee from Catholic High, invited me to a CYO dance. He arranged a blind

189

date for me with Emma Lane, a nice, attractive girl from St. Joseph's Academy. Only one problem: she was almost a foot taller than I.

We had to stop on the way to the dance to pick up a young thing whose date worked at the Paramount Theater and who would meet her at the function after his shift.

When we danced slowly, it was a little suggestive for me to nestle my forehead on Emma's neck, but when I danced with Shirley (before her date arrived) everything was perfect – her height, her smile, her laughter, personality, obvious purity, good looks and confidence. In a gym with one small window fan in Baton Rouge in August, she didn't perspire, I think because she felt it was unseemly.

We dated in November for an LSU game. I wanted to bet her a kiss that LSU would score on a particular play. If I won, which was unlikely, I would collect. If I lost, she would have to. Old ploy. She refused. She was smart, too.

She says she knew the first time we met. I wasn't far behind. I had it bad.

In September of '53, I proposed, she accepted and we approached her parents for a June, '54 wedding. After a long, long, looooong discussion, they agreed. In a few weeks, they reconsidered. We stood firm. They relented.

Since we had approval for June, why not try for semester break in February. Surprisingly, they agreed. Our priest at Christ the King Chapel on the LSU campus had met with her parents and had convinced them that although we were young (20 and 18), he felt we were ready. He had taught Shirley the marriage course at St. Joseph's.

Heck, why not at Christmas break of '53? With a formal church engagement service behind us, they were defenseless. We were married the day after Christmas. When we returned from our honeymoon, we had $80.00 between us; I was a sophomore in college.

In 2003, we celebrate our 50th. After seven pregnancies, four wonderful children, 15 great (in the superlative sense) grandchildren, a whirlwind career, 25 domiciles in four states, I wish to publicly thank Norris and Emma.

But mostly, I'd like to thank Shirley, a special kind of lady who has stood by boldly and confidently when often we received no income for many months at a time. She has been happy with however little or much we've had.

She has acquiesced with most of my investment projects, contributing considerably with the right kinds of questions and sobering advice. In fact, if I had listened to her reservations regarding some of my wildest harebrained programs, no telling how much better off we'd be, but she stood by her little man. I like to tease her saying that she won't ever leave me because if she did, I'd simply go with her, so what would be the use?

Our lives together have been free and wonderful. Few couples get to spend so much time together and survive the experience. Since 1976, I've been working at home, proof to me that we not only love each other, we love being together. Being with her and her inherent goodness makes me feel closer to God.

It takes a special kind of woman. Why me, Lord?

A Half Century of Love: Shirley!

Shirley and her pet goose, Maxine, revel in an early fall snow. Note the aspen leaves have not yet fallen completely.

Our prodigious progeny (Left to right, top to bottom for families and within families):
_ Derrec, Kelly, Mike holding Karly; Brian, Seanna, Myron III holding Logan, Matt, Jessica (inset).
_ Ryan, Christian, Lindsey, Debbie, Tim.
_ Jay and Brent holding Nicholas; Janet and Michelle holding Sarah.
_ Lana, Brent, Anne, Addie.

About the Author:

This is not Myron Tassin's first book; he has written/co-written over 20, facilitating a life of freedom between Colorado mountain cabins and Florida seaside cottages. Subjects have ranged from architecture to Mardi Gras; Proud, Peculiar New Orleans; the steam boating era; street cars, sports heroes, Arabian horses, the Grand Ole Opry and the Acadians.

Selected as LSU's "Outstanding Male Graduate in Journalism" in 1956, he chose a career in publishing-management, founded three firms and edited eight professional and trade journals, one with a national audience of 40,000. He wrote 56 programs for Mutual Sports.

In 1968, he co-authored his first book and – at age 70 – promises himself that this is the final one.

Printed in the United States
1360300008B/101-117